JAMES H. STRONGE

PAMELA D. TUCKER

JENNIFER L. HINDMAN

Handbook
for QUALITIES
of Effective
Teachers

ASCD

Association for Supervision
and Curriculum Development

Alexandria, Virginia USA

Association for Supervision and Curriculum Development
1703 N. Beauregard St. • Alexandria, VA 22311-1714 USA
Phone: 800-933-2723 or 703-578-9600 • Fax: 703-575-5400
Web site: www.ascd.org • E-mail: member@ascd.org
Author guidelines: www.ascd.org/write

Gene R. Carter, *Executive Director;* Nancy Modrak, *Director of Publishing;* Julie Houtz, *Director of Book Editing &*
Production; Deborah Siegel, *Project Manager;* Georgia Park, *Senior Graphic Designer;* Cynthia Stock, *Typesetter;*
Tracey A. Franklin, *Production Manager*

All Web links in this book are correct as of the publication date below but may have become inactive or otherwise modified since that time. If you notice a deactivated or changed link, please e-mail books@ascd.org with
the words "Link Update" in the subject line. In your message, please specify the Web link, the book title, and the
page number on which the link appears.

Paperback ISBN: 1-4166-0010-8 • ASCD product 104135 • List Price: $29.95 ($22.95 ASCD member price,
direct from ASCD only)   s12/04
e-books ($29.95): retail PDF ISBN: 1-4166-0182-1 • netLibrary ISBN: 1-4166-0180-5 •
ebrary ISBN: 1-4166-0181-3

Quantity discounts for this book: 10–49 copies, 10%; 50+ copies, 15%; for 500 or more copies,
call 800-933-2723, ext. 5634, or 703-575-5634.

10 09 08 07 06 05 04   12 11 10 9 8 7 6 5 4 3 2 1

To Mrs. Joan Palestini, my fifth grade teacher
James H. Stronge

To my children,
who provide a window on the many dimensions
of what it means to be a good teacher
Pamela D. Tucker

To Barry, who has taught me much
Jennifer L. Hindman

And

To the teachers who strive to make a profound
and positive impact on the lives of students every day
and to their administrators who are indispensable in
creating and supporting quality schools and schooling

Handbook for QUALITIES of Effective Teachers

ACKNOWLEDGMENTS

This writing endeavor is the result of many projects, studies, and prior undertakings involving many individuals. Each of these people contributed in meaningful ways to our understanding of what it means to be an effective teacher. Through countless workshops, we have heard teachers, principals, and superintendents ask:

What is an effective teacher?

▲ How do you help good teachers become even better?

▲ What tools and techniques are available to support and sustain quality teaching?

The *Handbook for Qualities of Effective Teachers* is our way of beginning to address these complex and profoundly important questions.

We appreciate the support from individuals at ASCD, in particular, Scott Willis, who recognized the value in the earlier work, *Qualities of Effective Teachers,* and gave us the opportunity to expand upon it.

Colleagues such as Barbara Howard and Wendy McColskey of SERVE at the University of North Carolina, Greensboro, offered invaluable support through our collaborative research on effective teachers. In particular, a research study regarding National Board for Professional Teaching Standards offered us the opportunity to build on our previous work and to improve and field test some of the forms included in this book.

We would like to acknowledge our graduate students at the College of William and Mary and the University of Virginia who helped us better understand the complexities of teaching in today's schools.

We especially would like to acknowledge the contribution of the dedicated practitioners mentioned above with whom we have interacted in numerous workshops and professional development institutes. You have asked the fundamental questions that drive this discussion about quality teachers and have helped us explore the complexities of assisting others as they strive to improve their practice. Finally, thank you to all the readers whose desire to bridge research and practice made this book possible.

INTRODUCTION: MAXIMIZING YOUR USE OF THE HANDBOOK

Most teachers do not want to be just good teachers, they want to be great teachers.

NWREL, 2001, p. 18

The *Handbook*, simply put, is about supporting quality teachers. It is presented as a companion to the book *Qualities of Effective Teachers* (Stronge, 2002). Whereas *Qualities of Effective Teachers* is intended to provide a readable, user-friendly synthesis of research regarding what it means to be an effective teacher, the *Handbook* is designed to provide the ways and means for applying the research.

As teachers grow professionally, their instructional expertise increases, and they become more effective at various aspects of teaching. They have a greater repertoire of instructional, management, and assessment knowledge and skills from which to draw as they create meaningful student learning experiences. Our intent with the *Handbook for Qualities of Effective Teachers* is to provide a tool for teachers as they seek to improve their effectiveness in delivering high-quality, productive learning experiences for all students.

We trust that the tools and techniques included in the *Handbook* will prove to be practical and user-friendly in supporting effective teachers. Regardless of how effective any one of us might be in our teaching, we can continue to grow and improve. For master teachers, the *Handbook* is aimed at continual improvement and sustaining quality teaching. For others, the tools are designed to help identify areas for performance improvement, and to focus support for the important and ongoing process of development. As with the original *Qualities* book, our ultimate goal is to improve the educational experiences and achievement of the students we serve in our schools by focusing directly on teacher effectiveness.

Organization of the *Handbook*

The *Handbook* provides tools that can be selected by teachers, peer coaches, principals, supervisors, and others to focus on improving teacher performance. Each chapter is organized around the six qualities introduced in the *Qualities* book:

▲ Prerequisites of effective teachers,

▲ The teacher as a person,

▲ Classroom management and organization,

▲ Organizing for instruction,

▲ Implementing instruction, and

▲ Monitoring student progress and potential.

Each chapter contains two graphic organizers. The first appears shortly after the chapter introduction and provides a visual overview of the key indicators associated with each quality. The figure below shows the general format that is replicated in each chapter.

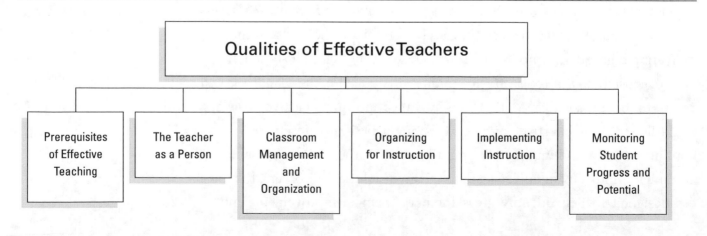

The second graphic organizer is at the end of the chapter. Each organizer differs in format (depending on the quality being discussed) to demonstrate various examples of graphic organizers.

Chapter 1 investigates prerequisites of effective teaching, focusing on the influence of background and professional training on teacher effectiveness. The chapter provides tools for examining and improving verbal ability and content knowledge and discusses teacher education and experience.

Chapter 2 examines what the effective teacher is like as a person, focusing on the importance of caring, fairness and respect, social interactions with students, promotion of enthusiasm and motivation for learning, attitude toward the teaching profession, and reflective practice. This chapter highlights strategies for assessing and reflecting upon these qualities.

Chapter 3 provides guidance related to the management and organizational skills an effective teacher displays. The qualities and assessment tools highlighted in this chapter address using classroom management skills, applying elements of organization, and managing and responding to student behavior.

Chapter 4 offers tools related to organizing for instruction. Specific qualities discussed include focusing on instruction, maximizing instructional time, expecting students to achieve, and planning and preparing for instruction.

Chapter 5 focuses on the actual process of implementing instruction. Of particular interest are the qualities of using instructional strategies, communicating high expectations to students, understanding the complexities of teaching, using questioning techniques, and supporting student engagement in learning.

Chapter 6 presents a number of approaches to gauging effectiveness related to monitoring student progress and potential. Specific qualities highlighted in the chapter are the importance of homework, monitoring student learning and providing feedback, and responding to the range of student needs and abilities in the classroom.

Each chapter includes a parallel set of features, which focus on teacher effectiveness. These features are

▲ A teacher scenario that highlights the particular quality presented in the chapter.

▲ A brief review of research supporting each quality.

▲ "Visualizing the Quality," which is a graphic organizer relating the key quality indicators introduced in the chapter.

▲ "Focus on the Teacher," which introduces and applies tools for teacher improvement.

▲ "Making Connections," which asks readers to consider the fictitious teacher's positive attributes and areas for improvement. The section also asks readers to reflect on their own professional practice.

▲ The "Resources" section, which includes two features: 1) the "Author's Perspective," which provides suggested answers to the questions posed in the "Focus on the Teacher" section; and 2) blackline masters that can be photocopied and used in your own practice. In some chapters additional tables are added to this section to elaborate on an idea presented within the chapter.

Uses for the *Handbook*

The *Handbook for Qualities of Effective Teachers* aims to improve the quality of teacher performance and the resulting learning opportunities for students. We have endeavored to develop a wealth of approaches for capturing and analyzing the endless facets of teaching in different circumstances and with different purposes and students. In this effort we trust the book can be a valuable resource for

▲ *teachers* who desire to enhance their own performance through reflection and application of tools for improving performance;

▲ *teacher leaders* who are engaged in mentoring and collaborative schoolwide improvement;

▲ *instructional coaches* who are actively supporting the critical work of teachers;

▲ *school administrators* who supervise and evaluate teachers;

▲ *staff development specialists* who plan and deliver training focused on improving and sustaining quality instruction;

▲ *human resource specialists* who are responsible for selecting and retaining high-quality teacher applicants;

▲ *teacher and administrator educators* who can employ the book's research and application strategies in their teacher training and instructional leadership programs, respectively; and

▲ *policymakers* and their staffs who are responsible for developing tools and strategies for state or district teacher development and evaluation processes.

We offer our best wishes and sincere hopes for success as you continue your important work of building, supporting, and sustaining teacher effectiveness.

PREREQUISITES OF EFFECTIVE TEACHING

Maria Ortez graduated from college 10 years ago with a double major in journalism and history. She has returned to the rural community where she grew up to be closer to her parents and siblings and lead a quieter life. Before coming back, she worked as a reporter for several newspapers, including the biggest one in the state. Maria is interested in teaching, and she had a great interview with the principal, department chair, and parent representative. The high school is excited to have someone with real-world knowledge of journalism teach the elective class. Maria also will be teaching three classes of U.S. History. Before deciding to hire Maria, the department chair and the principal spoke about the types of support Maria would need. It is now the end of the first marking period, and while it is clear that Maria knows her content, her teaching skills are weak.

Research Summary

Effective teaching is a continual learning process, and each school year brings changes to which competent teachers must adapt. Changes can happen in terms of students, curriculum, building issues, colleagues, administrators, finances, health and safety concerns, families, communities, and a host of other influences on the daily lives of teachers. The foundation upon which teachers base their ability to adapt to changes and successfully navigate the complexities of the classroom comes largely from their personal abilities and experiences. These personal abilities and experiences can be classified as prerequisites to teaching—that is, competencies that are acquired and demonstrated before the teacher ever walks through the schoolhouse door. Prerequisites of effective teaching are often considered in relation to novice teachers, but in fact they reflect the accumulated competencies and experiences that any teacher brings to the classroom. Research suggests that the following prerequisites are linked to effective teachers:

▲ *Verbal Ability* has a positive effect on student achievement (Darling-Hammond, 2000; Haberman, 1995; Hanushek, 1971).

▲ *Content Knowledge* as measured by majoring or minoring in the subject area or participating in professional development in the content contributes to increased student learning (Fetler, 1999; Wenglinsky, 2000).

▲ *Educational Coursework* is a stronger predictor of teaching effectiveness than grade point average or test scores (Ferguson & Womack, 1993). For teachers who embrace the concept of life-long learning, continued professional development in their field results in increased student achievement (Wenglinsky, 2002).

▲ *Teacher Certification,* regardless of the type of certification held, results in teachers being more effective than their uncertified counterparts (Darling-Hammond, 2000; Darling-Hammond, Berry, & Thoreson, 2001; Goldhaber & Brewer, 2000; Hawk, Coble, & Swanson, 1985).

▲ *Teaching Experience,* up to a point, is influential in teacher effectiveness, particularly in the areas of planning, classroom management, questioning, and reflection (Covino & Iwanicki, 1996; Fetler, 1999; Reynolds, 1992).

The prerequisites discussed in this chapter focus on the professional aspects of what teachers bring to their work and do not include the personal characteristics of effective teachers that will be discussed in the next chapter. Figure 1.1 provides a visual overview of this chapter. Following an elaboration of the five key quality indicators associated with prerequisites of effective teaching, tools to enhance effectiveness are presented in the context of our fictional teacher, Maria. The questions posed in the *Focus on the Teacher* section are addressed at the end of the chapter before the presentation of the blackline masters.

FIGURE 1.1

Chapter Overview

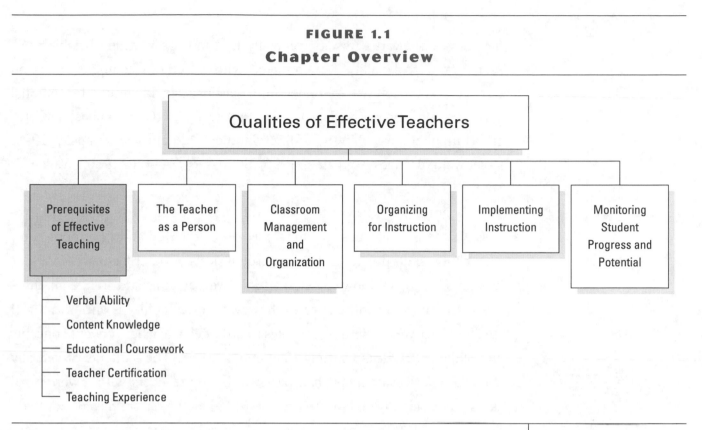

Verbal Ability

Teachers make connections with their students, colleagues, and students' families through words and actions. Effective teachers know their students and how to communicate with them, both individually and collectively. Some students prefer "just the facts" while others want to hear a narrative, and then there are others with completely different learning styles and communication needs. Effective teachers carefully consider their audience when delivering a message. They observe reactions and decide how best to get their point across to different individuals.

The connection between teacher effectiveness and verbal ability is not new (Hanushek, 1971). Indeed, this finding simply verifies what people already know: the ability of teachers to effectively communicate influences the relationships they establish with others, the clarity of explanations to students, and, invariably, student understanding and achievement. While studies regarding the relationship between verbal ability and teacher effectiveness have produced varied results, generally the findings indicate that high test scores on verbal ability are associated with effective teaching. Studies on teachers' verbal ability have drawn from various tests, including the National Teacher Examination (NTE), Graduate Record Exam (GRE), Praxis, and others (Ehrenberg, & Brewer, 1995; Gitomer, Latham, & Ziomek, 1999; Greenwald, Hedges, & Laine, 1996; Strauss & Sawyer, 1986; Wayne & Youngs, 2003).

Of course, high verbal test scores are not necessarily proof of effectiveness. Obviously, it is possible for someone to test well and have poor communication skills due to poor interpersonal skills or other factors; conversely, it is possible to get a low score on a test of verbal skills and still be an effective communicator. In most cases, however, verbal ability is an indicator of teacher effectiveness because it relates to how well a teacher conveys concepts and skills to students (Darling-Hammond, 2001). The students of verbally adept teachers learn more than peers taught by teachers with lower verbal skills (Haycock, 2000; Rowan, Chiang, & Miller, 1997; Thomas B. Fordham Foundation, 1999). When students understand what teachers are communicating, and when teachers understand the signals from their students, a two-way communication process is created that enhances the learning of students. Consequently, as a general rule, effective communicators are likely to be more effective teachers.

Content Knowledge

Teachers cannot teach what they don't know. The research clearly shows that teachers (particularly in the areas of mathematics and science) who have majored or minored in the subject area they teach attain better achievement results with their students than teachers without background in their subject areas (Wenglinsky, 2000). For example, a California study found that mathematics teachers who had a major or a minor in mathematics had students with higher test scores on the Stanford 9 Achievement test (Fetler, 1999).

The relationship between teacher knowledge and student acquisition of knowledge makes sense. Successful teachers know the content and can determine the essential knowledge and skills that are necessary for mastery of the subject in order to integrate them into effective instruction (Langer, 2001). They can better convey their enthusiasm, understanding, and knowledge to students. These knowledgeable teachers also are better able to connect the "real world" to the topics addressed in the curriculum. Furthermore, the better job teachers do in teaching important subject-specific concepts and skills, the more likely it is that students will be able to access the material in the future—for example on a standardized test—or to transfer the information to a related situation or topic (Popham, 1999). Because people tend to study a topic in which they are interested in greater depth, those with a greater content knowledge tend to be more enthusiastic about their subject, and they can better engage the learner during the presentation of the lesson.

Effective teachers organize and present content knowledge and skills to students in a manner that helps the students access, interact with, and learn the material. Additionally, students value teachers who effectively convey their knowledge of the subject area through strong communication skills (NASSP, 1997; Peart & Campbell, 1999). One benefit of content-area preparation may be that teachers with a major or minor in a subject are more likely to attend professional development offerings in that area and incorporate application skills into instruction (Wenglinsky, 2002). In the final analysis, effective teachers have deep understanding and respect for their content area. Furthermore, they become experts in sharing their subject with their students in meaningful ways.

Educational Coursework

The research addressing educational coursework typically refers to the courses teachers took as part of their preparation program for teaching or as a part of postgraduate work to earn their teacher certification, but educational coursework does not stop with the signing of a teaching contract. Teachers must continue to develop their professional knowledge in order to renew their licenses and, perhaps more importantly, to renew themselves. For many teachers, this renewal entails taking graduate classes in education, attending conferences, and participating in a myriad of other professional development opportunities. What teachers do in terms of acquiring knowledge and skills, both before and after they begin teaching, influences the learning that occurs in their classrooms.

The value of educational coursework versus content-area study is often debated. We don't advocate one instead of the other; in fact, both are critically important to effective teaching. The pedagogical courses that teachers take before entering the classroom influence their ability to convey curriculum and content to students and assess its acquisition. After studying 266 student teachers, researchers concluded that increasing subject-area coursework and decreasing education-related work would be counterproductive as there is a link between student achievement and teacher education coursework (Ferguson & Womack, 1993). Educational coursework provides a framework for effective teaching. Typically, it encompasses planning, assessment, classroom management, student development, and instructional pedagogy.

Teacher preparation is offered in a variety of formats, ranging from traditional four-year college preparatory programs to postgraduate alternative programs. One key element is methods classes that teach future educators how to package subject matter and skills into quality learning experiences, instruction, and assessment, as well as exposing future teachers to how students learn (Berliner, 1986; Scherer, 2001). Furthermore, education majors are initially better at lesson planning, classroom management, and instructional differentiation than their counterparts who did not have teaching preparation (Ferguson & Womack, 1993). This preparation typically results in higher levels of student achievement; additionally teachers who graduated from five-year programs tend to be more effective than graduates of four-year education programs (Darling-Hammond, 2000). Other findings include the following:

▲ Education courses in math and science methods positively correlate to student achievement in those subjects (Monk, 1994).

▲ Students whose teachers took courses in teaching methods are likely to perform better than students whose teachers did not (Wenglinsky, 2002).

▲ For math teachers, education methods courses had more powerful effects on student achievement than merely taking more courses in the content area (Monk, 1994).

Teachers continue to develop throughout their careers as they learn the science and art of teaching. When educators participate in professional development offerings that relate to the content area or population of students they teach, it enhances their effectiveness, resulting in higher levels of student academic success (Camphire, 2001; Cross & Regden, 2002). Enhancing the quality of professional development by linking it to teacher goals results in improved teacher effectiveness (Danielson, 2001; Guskey, 2002). For example, science teachers with professional development in laboratory skills have students who out-perform their peers (Wenglinsky, 2000). The same study found that teachers who received staff development in how to work with diverse students or higher-order thinking skills had students who performed better on the National Assessment of Educational Progress (Wenglinsky, 2000).

Professional development should focus on what teachers need to do and accomplish in the school and with their students (Schalock, Schalock, & Myton, 1998). For example, professional development in instructional differentiation makes a difference in student achievement as teachers are better able to meet diverse students' needs (Rowan, Chiang, & Miller, 1997; Tomlinson, 1999; Wenglinsky, 2000). A relationship exists between learning practices and what strategies teachers know; thus, teachers need the opportunity to work with others (e.g., coaches, mentors, experts) to enhance teacher effectiveness through sharing as this provides a forum for collaboration and renewal (Darling-Hammond, 2001; Hoff, 2000). Another area of professional development that improves effectiveness is cultural competence, especially if the teacher is from a different background than the students he or she is teaching (Sleeter, 2001). Enhancing professional skills helps teachers feel empowered to make changes aimed at enhancing learning experiences that, in turn, result in better student retention, attendance, and academic success (see, for example, Blair, 2000; Lin, 2002; Wenglinsky, 2002). Obviously, teachers grow when they have the opportunity to acquire knowledge and skills that they can use in the classroom. This growth often contributes to the acquisition of points, credits, or units that are necessary to maintain teacher licensure, which will be addressed in the next section.

Teacher Certification

Teacher certification is determined by individual states and is issued to individuals whom the state deems qualified to teach based on its criteria. In most states, proper certification or licensure is the operational definition of a "highly qualified teacher" as required in *No Child Left Behind*. Although being certified does not necessarily guarantee effectiveness, students of certified teachers typically do have higher levels of achievement than do students of uncertified teachers (Darling-Hammond, 2000; Darling-Hammond, et al., 2001; Goldhaber & Brewer, 2000; Hawk, et al., 1985; Laczko-Kerr & Berliner, 2002). For example, in one study, teachers who were certified increased their students' achievement by a grade equivalency of two months (20 percent) over their uncertified counterparts (Laczko-Kerr & Berliner). Thus, effective educators tend to be certified in their teaching field, resulting in higher levels of student achievement on standardized tests (Glass, 2002). This finding has serious implications for urban and high-poverty schools, which tend to have more difficulty in recruiting and retaining fully certified teachers (Wayne & Youngs, 2003).

There are multiple routes to earning teacher certification, ranging from traditional preparation programs to abbreviated alternative ones like Teach for America, with a host of intermediate options. Most states have some form of alternative certification that allows individuals who have a bachelor's degree to earn their certification without getting an advanced degree in education or taking additional undergraduate courses. The results of studies on the effects of alternative licensure programs are mixed (Qu & Becker, 2003). Some findings indicate that alternatively prepared and certified teachers are just as effective as their traditionally prepared counterparts (Miller, McKenna, & McKenna, 1998), while others report that these teachers are not as well prepared to meet the challenges of the classroom (Jelmberg, 1996; Laczko-Kerr & Berliner, 2002). In a study comparing graduates of traditional and alternative routes offered at the same university, it was found that there was no difference in student achievement based on the format in which the teachers received their educational coursework (Miller, McKenna, & McKenna, 1998). On the other hand, a relatively recent study found that after controlling for students' pretest scores and teachers' degrees and experience, teachers with temporary or emergency certification had lower achievement than more experienced and traditionally prepared teachers (Darling-Hammond, Berry, & Thoreson, 2001). A subsequent study that compared teachers who had earned their certification in a traditional program to those with emergency certification found that traditionally certified teachers outperformed teachers with emergency licenses (Qu & Becker). Certification does make a difference, but it is just one piece of the much larger puzzle of teacher quality.

For certification to be considered as a quality indicator, teachers should be assigned to teach in their field of study (Wayne & Youngs, 2003). In an investigation of 359 secondary teachers whose schools were being reorganized to reduce the emphasis on departments, researchers found that teachers had a decreased sense of efficacy when assigned out of field (Ross, Cousins, Gadalla, & Hannay, 1999). This finding illustrates the impact on educators when they are asked to instruct in an area outside of their area of training. A matched-pairs study comparing certified teachers who were licensed to teach mathematics to those licensed in another area found that students taught by teachers instructing in their field of preparation had higher levels of achievement (Hawk, Coble, & Swanson, 1985). Furthermore, the study found that teachers assigned in their field scored higher on measures of instructional presentation and content knowledge. Additional research established that teachers who are licensed in the area in which they are teaching have higher student achievement in reading and mathematics than out-of-field teachers (Darling-Hammond, 2001). In summary, teacher certification enhances effectiveness so long as teachers are assigned to teach in their field of preparation.

Teaching Experience

There is no firm agreement in the research literature regarding how many years make a teacher "experienced." For the purposes of effectiveness, the range appears to be between three and eight years as the point when teachers are first identified as "experienced" (Sanders, 2001; Scherer, 2001). Moreover, the relationship between teaching experience and teacher effectiveness is not always linear and tends to plateau before declining (Darling-Hammond, 2000; Sanders, 2001).

Experience does make a difference in teacher effectiveness, as it offers teachers the opportunity to grow professionally by learning from practice. This growth is a part of the learning curve that novice teachers experience as they begin their transformation into competent teachers. Consequently, students of experienced teachers tend to have higher levels of achievement (Fetler, 1999; Glass, 2002; Wenglinsky, 2000). Negative effects on student achievement have been associated with the proportion of beginning teachers to whom students are assigned (Betts, Rueben, & Dannenberg, 2000; Fetler, 1999; Goe, 2002). Couple this finding with the fact that inexperienced teachers are disproportionately located in academically needy schools, and a troubling pattern emerges (Darling-Hammond, 1995).

For teachers who are in collegial settings, experience tends to help those teachers improve throughout their careers (Darling-Hammond, 2000). The key benefits of experience are that the teacher has time to

▲ develop an increased depth of understanding about the content and how to teach it to students (Covino & Iwanicki, 1996),

▲ learn and use various strategies to meet students' needs (Durall, 1995; Glass, 2001),

▲ learn how to maximize his or her usage of instructional materials, management of the classroom, and working relationships with others (Reynolds, 1992), and

▲ incorporate reflective practice (Allen & Casbergue, 2000).

Visualizing the Quality

We have used a type of graphic organizer called *webbing* to visually represent plausible relationships among the prerequisites of effective teaching (Figure 1.2). For most teachers, this would be the likely order of acquired qualities, but we recognize that by creating a linear web, we have oversimplified the relationships. Verbal abilities would affect someone's acquisition and mastery of both educational coursework and content knowledge, which together

FIGURE 1.2

**Visual Representation of Prerequisites
to Effective Teaching (example of clustering)**

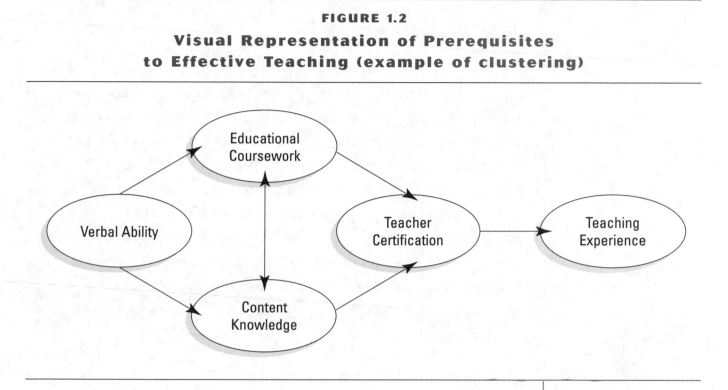

would be prerequisites for teacher certification. The cumulative development of these prerequisites would set the stage for gaining teaching experience.

Focus on the Teacher

Maria is an intelligent woman who made a positive impression on the interview team. She has begun to take steps toward satisfying the requirements for a permanent teaching license and has been in contact with the human resources director (who also handles licensing issues) about the process. When the school year started, Maria was teaching on an emergency certificate, but she was also enrolled in a distance-learning program to complete the coursework necessary to obtain a secondary license in history. The school provided Maria with a mentor and some additional supports.

The tools presented in this section of the chapter can be useful in helping teachers like Maria become more effective. The forms include a teacher inventory, a form for personal improvement and goal setting, and a form for teacher reflection.

Teacher Inventory

A teacher inventory process can be used by an administrator, mentor, instructional coach, or the teacher who is new to the school to identify the assets, needs, and possible actions that will need to be taken to ensure a smooth transition into the new setting. The inventory draws on all of the information available to the individuals who have interviewed and met with the beginning teacher. To illustrate, the principal and department chair completed the form in Figure 1.3 in an effort to target their induction efforts. The form starts with the teacher's assets as it often is easy to overlook the reasons a person was hired if the deficiency list becomes too long. The form also can be used reflectively by teachers who are transitioning to a new grade level, school, or content area as a way of analyzing the strengths and weaknesses they bring to that position.

Personal Improvement Goal Setting

Goal setting is a strategy that is often used in combination with teacher evaluation or as an alternative to traditional observation for more accomplished teachers. The purpose of personal improvement goal setting is to focus attention on professional or instructional improvement based on a process of determining baseline performance, developing goals, identifying strategies for improvement, and assessing results at the end of the plan's time period. Various authors have proposed that people are motivated by their personal goals and, thus, a key strategy in performance improvement is to assist in the shaping and focusing of those goals to align with schoolwide and systemwide initiatives. Given the flexibility of goal setting, it can be implemented with the whole spectrum of teachers, from novice to experienced and from accomplished to struggling, depending on its focus and structure. For new teachers, goal setting may need to be more prescriptive and goal attainment may be fundamental to their success as novice teachers.

Most goal-setting models involve five basic components:

1. Identification of a focus or need;
2. Description of baseline data relevant to the focus or need;

FIGURE 1.3
Teacher Inventory

Directions: Reflect on what is known about the teacher. Identify what talents, abilities, and knowledge the individual possesses that will be assets to the school and its students, and place these in the *Assets* column. Next, consider the needs or potential weaknesses that the teacher has and place them in the appropriate column. Finally, brainstorm possible actions you could take: professional experiences or available resources that could make a difference in this teacher's performance.

Assets	Needs	Possible Actions
Has real-life experience as a reporter	Everything related to instructional pedagogy and classroom management	Schedule Maria's planning time to coincide with her mentor's, maybe Mr. Andrews
Has a major in history	• Sense of classroom discipline	
Knows the community	• How to provide and maintain a robust learning environment	See if Mrs. Craig (special education) would be willing to co-teach with Maria second period. This would give her a model every day of what great instruction looks like and would be a smaller class (disadvantage is that Maria is brand new and this may be intimidating—the positive is that she'd pick up an extra planning period to collaborate with Mrs. Craig as there would be no homeroom).
Is willing to take courses to earn certification . . . she initiated this	• Understanding of planning for instruction (although, she has done it for writing)	
	• Instructional strategies	
Has passed the Praxis I test . . . done prior to applying (showed forethought)	• Student assessment	
	To trust that we are here to support her and that it is okay to ask for help.	
Is able to connect with people	Certification	Do not assign Maria to extra duties and explain to her that we don't expect her to assume any . . . she has enough to learn right now.
Has done public speaking with her job as a reporter to various groups	Mentor	
Respects deadlines	Time to observe others, meet with teachers, etc.	Department chair will meet with her to discuss goal setting for personal improvement.
Was very confident in her desire to share her love of journalism and history		

◄

Reflect on the Teacher: Case 1A

What other assets, needs, and possible actions would you add to the table?

Under possible actions, the principal and department chair were thinking about how to get Maria additional support through co-teaching. They started to consider pro/cons. What do you think they should decide?

3. Articulation of a goal or goals;

4. Listing of strategies for achieving the goal (resources, training, etc); and

5. Documentation of results and/or evaluation.

Developing meaningful goals is the cornerstone of the goal-setting process. Unless personal improvement goals are useful and worthy, it doesn't matter if they are or are not attained. Moreover, useful and worthy goals take considerable effort to formulate. One way to focus the goal is to define a specific outcome indicator, such as an assessment strategy or type of performance, and set a clear and measurable target performance. Figure 1.4 shows Maria's goal for the school year.

FIGURE 1.4

Annual Goal for Personal Improvement

Teacher Maria Ortez   **School** Merryville High School

Grade/Subject 11th/U.S. History   **Administrator** Mr. Cline

                                                                           School Year 2003–2004

Setting *[Describe the population and special learning circumstances.]*
The high school has 849 students from the surrounding rural area that includes four small towns. Most of the students are deeply rooted in the area. Approximately 43 percent of the students participate in the free/reduced meal program. Each year, approximately 25 percent of the graduating class continues their education at the community college, university, or trade schools. The U.S. History class is required for all 11th graders.

My 84 U.S. History students represent the school population. I have three students who have special learning needs so I have to make sure to prepare their materials in advance.

Content Area *[The area/topic I will address (e.g., reading instruction, long division, problem solving).]*
Use of graphic organizers in U.S. History

Baseline Data *[Where I am now (i.e., status at beginning of year).]*
At the suggestion of my mentor, I gave the students a pre-assessment at the start of the school year. My mentor assisted me in making sense of the data. If that pre-assessment was correct, 9 students would have passed; another 30 would have been close.

The students have not had U.S. History since middle school. They know a disjointed bunch of facts and have little knowledge of how current world events often have their roots (particularly if conflict is involved) in the past.

Goal Statement *[What I want to accomplish this year (i.e., my desired results).]*
Students will use graphic organizers to relate key events and figures in U.S. History to present day-to-day happenings and demonstrate their understanding through:
   a) improved performance on appropriate subtests of the pre-assessment given as part of the midterm and semester final, and
   b) satisfactory performance on the state mandated end-of-course test given in May.

Strategies for Improvement *[Activities I will use to accomplish my goal.]*
  • Attend school district training on graphic organizers (early October offering)
  • Meet with my mentor teacher to collaborate on graphic organizers and relate them to the specific parts of the curriculum
  • Instruct students on the various types of organizers (introduce one every two weeks and reinforce it)

Evaluator's Signature/Date   Teacher's Signature/Date

End-of-Year Data/Results *[Accomplishments by year end.]*

Evaluator's Signature/Date   Teacher's Signature/Date

Adapted from: Stronge, J. H., & Tucker, P. D. (2003). *Handbook on Teacher Evaluation: Assessing and Improving Performance.* Larchmont, NY: Eye on Education.

Reflect on the Teacher: Case 1B

What is it about Maria's personal improvement goal that indicates that she might develop some of the strategies of an effective teacher?

Making Connections

Consider the Scenario

Reread the teacher scenario at the beginning of this chapter and the bits of information about Maria throughout the chapter. Think about the skills she has and the skills that she needs to improve.

Using the space below, consider the desirable characteristics that Maria has as a beginning teacher and what areas need improvement based on the five indicators of effective teaching presented in this chapter: verbal ability, content knowledge, educational coursework, teacher certification, and teaching experience.

Positive Attributes	Areas for Improvement

What descriptor best describes Maria's prerequisite skills for teaching?

____ Master: demonstrates the complexity of the qualities in this domain that likely will result in a rich learning experience for students

____ Professional: demonstrates the qualities in most areas, so there will be a productive learning experience for students

____ Apprentice: demonstrates the qualities well enough for learning to occur, but is likely to have specific and significant areas for improvement

____ Undeveloped: lacks sufficient skills and behaviors necessary to justify a renewed contract

Why did you select a particular descriptor?

How could Maria's performance be improved?

Reflecting on My Current Performance

Rate your own performance on the qualities associated with implementing instruction using the explanation of each major quality highlighted in the chapter.

Quality	Undeveloped	Apprentice	Professional	Master
Verbal Ability				
Content Knowledge				
Educational Coursework				
Teacher Certification				
Teaching Experience				

Reflection Learning Log

What do I better understand now after studying and reflecting on the prerequisites of effective teachers?

What are next steps to improve my performance?

What resources (e.g., people and materials) are needed to enhance my teaching effectiveness?

Resources

This section contains two items: 1) the *Authors' Perspective* and 2) *blackline masters* of forms that can be used to promote improvement and reflection on qualities of effective teachers.

Reflect on the Teacher: Authors' Perspective

The "Reflect on the Teacher" questions in this chapter are intended to encourage interactive and reflective reading and application of the ideas presented. In most cases, there are no precisely right or wrong answers. The "Authors' Perspective" is provided as one way to reflect on the information presented.

Reflect on the Teacher: Case 1A (see p. 19)

What other assets, needs, and possible actions would you add to the teacher inventory (figure 1.3)?

Answers will vary. Suggestions include:

- ▲ Assets: Makes a good first impression; willing to work hard to meet expectations for certification.
- ▲ Needs: fine tuning of the list under "everything related to instructional pedagogy and classroom management" focusing on skills that will have the greatest payoff for a beginning teacher.
- ▲ Possible Actions: assign her U.S. History classes that are all at the same level as opposed to a mixture of honors, regular, and remedial.

Under possible actions, the principal and department chair were thinking about how to get Maria additional support through co-teaching. They started to consider pro/cons. What do you think they should decide?

Co-teaching is a complex partnership in which both teachers need to determine how they want to plan, teach, and assess students. They should have shared expectations for student behavior and achievement when they are in the classroom together. If Mrs. Craig and Maria are to be partners, there is the potential for tension, because one knows what it is to be a teacher and the other is still developing an understanding. While Maria could offer her content knowledge, Mrs. Craig would be initially responsible for leading Maria through the ins and outs of not only co-teaching, but also teaching itself. There are definitely advantages to co-teaching, ranging from a lower student-to-teacher ratio to an opportunity to collaborate closely with another professional. While this is a novel way to get Maria additional support, co-teaching is complex. It should be planned, and both participants need to know they are partners and equally valued. Additionally, making a significant change in students' schedules may not be in everyone's best interests as this is now the end of the first marking period. Co-teaching would be a better option to implement at the beginning of the school year. For now, it might be better if Maria observed Mrs. Craig on occasion.

Reflect on the Teacher: Case 1B (see p. 21)

What aspects of Maria's personal improvement goal indicate that she might develop some of the strategies to be an effective teacher?

▲ Use of a pre-assessment. While her mentor suggested it and is supporting her in its development, Maria's awareness of its importance suggests her understanding that pre-assessments let teachers know where students are when they begin their work with them, so lessons can be attuned to students' needs and strengths.

▲ Desire to connect history to the "real world." Effective teachers seek to create meaningful learning experiences for students and link their prior knowledge to the new experiences.

Blackline Masters

The following blackline masters can be photocopied and used in your school or district.

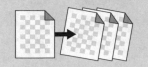

Teacher Profile Analysis —
Assets, Needs, and Possible Actions

Directions: Reflect on what is known about the teacher. Identify what talents, abilities, and knowledge the individual possesses that will be assets to the school and its students, and place these in the *Assets* column. Next, consider the needs or potential weaknesses that the teacher has and place them in the appropriate column. Finally, brainstorm possible actions you could take: professional experiences or available resources that could make a difference in this teacher's performance.

Assets	Needs	Possible Actions

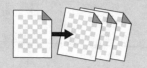

Teacher Annual Goal for Personal Improvement

Teacher_____ School_____

Grade/Subject_____ Administrator_____

School Year_____

Setting *[Describe the population and special learning circumstances.]*

Content Area *[The area/topic I will address (e.g., reading instruction, long division, problem solving).]*

Baseline Data *[Where I am now (i.e., status at beginning of year).]*

Goal Statement *[What I want to accomplish this year (i.e., my desired results).]*

Strategies for Improvement *[Activities I will use to accomplish my goal.]*

_____   _____
Administrator's Signature/Date   Teacher's Signature/Date

Mid-Year Data/Results *[What progress has been made]*

Modifications *[Revisions needed to the strategies to accomplish the goal]*

_____   _____
Administrator's Signature/Date   Teacher's Signature/Date

End-of-Year Data/Results *[Accomplishments by year end]*

Considerations *[Thoughts, reflection on next steps for next year]*

_____   _____
Administrator's Signature/Date   Teacher's Signature/Date

Adapted from: Stronge, J. H., & Tucker, P. D. (2003). *Handbook on Teacher Evaluation: Assessing and Improving Performance.* Larchmont, NY: Eye on Education.

THE TEACHER AS A PERSON

Barbara Wells is an experienced teacher who came to an ethnically diverse school because her husband was transferred to the area. Her previous principal commented in the letter of recommendation that Barbara had been an asset to the suburban school in which she had taught. However, the teachers on Barbara's grade level team at this new middle school have noticed that she doesn't seem to understand the students or their families and she is having difficulty establishing relationships in the classroom and beyond.

Research Summary

Are people born to be teachers? Can people develop into effective teachers? Are there people who should never be teachers? With some qualification, perhaps the answer to each question is yes. Teaching is a vocation for which some people have a natural talent while others may have the inclination but need to develop some of the necessary skills, and others simply may not be suited to the demands of the role. We do know that the most effective teachers are passionate about their chosen profession. *The Teacher as a Person* chapter is the most person-centered chapter in the book. It goes beyond classroom management, instruction, and assessment to investigate the affective aspects of teaching. When people are asked about their best teachers, they often recount how the teacher made them feel before mentioning how much they learned. It is a subtle yet important distinction. A teacher's interpersonal skills are the basis for creating strong working relationships and a positive classroom climate for learning (Wubbels, Levy, & Brekelmans, 1997). Individuals remember the relationships, and those relationships can be powerful motivators to learning.

We know that some teachers may be effective with a particular group of students and not with others. However, our premise is that truly effective teachers are good with all students in their particular subject or grade level, assuming the teachers have the necessary training for the given teaching assignment. There are six key indicators associated with this quality of *Teacher as a Person*. It can be argued that some of these characteristics cannot be taught, only modeled. We suggest that building awareness regarding the importance of each of these key quality indicators is a first step in the development process, to be followed by modeling and feedback. The indicators associated with *The Teacher as a Person* are caring, fairness and respect, attitude toward the teaching profession, social interactions with students, promotion of enthusiasm and motivation for learning, and reflective practice.

- ▲ *Caring* can be demonstrated in many ways by teachers but, at its core, caring means teachers understand and value students as unique individuals (Noddings, 1984, 1992; Peart & Campbell, 1999).
- ▲ *Fairness and Respect* involves treating students in a balanced and open-minded manner that is considerate of their circumstances. This quality has been called the foundation of effective teaching (Collinson, Killeavy, & Stephenson, 1999).
- ▲ *Attitude Toward the Teaching Profession* is undoubtedly the pivotal quality that determines a teacher's willingness to develop and grow as a professional. The more positive and enthusiastic teachers are about teaching, the more likely their students will be enthusiastic about learning (Edmonton Public Schools, 1993).
- ▲ *Social Interactions with Students* can take place within the classroom but also beyond—for example, during sporting events and other special programs. When teachers demonstrate interest in students' lives

outside of the classroom, students are encouraged to perform their best in the classroom (Kohn, 1996). Humor, caring, respect, and fairness all are involved in building relationships with students (Peart & Campbell, 1999).

▲ ***Promotion of Enthusiasm and Motivation for Learning*** by the teacher results in higher levels of student involvement and achievement (Darling-Hammond, 2001). Effective teachers encourage students to work and reach their potential.

▲ ***Reflective Practice*** is the process by which all professionals develop expertise. It is by analysis of our actions and their effects on others that we learn from experience and move along the continuum from novice to expert teachers (Thomas & Montgomery, 1998).

The above sampling of findings demonstrates the complexity of teaching as an interpersonal activity. Figure 2.1 provides a visual overview of this chapter. Following an elaboration of the six key quality indicators associated

FIGURE 2.1
Chapter Overview

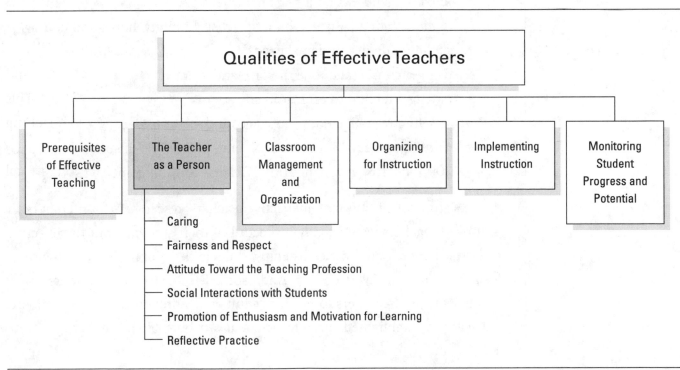

with the quality of *Teacher as a Person*, tools to enhance effectiveness in this area are presented based on our fictional teacher, Barbara. The questions posed in the *Focus on the Teacher* section are addressed at the end of the chapter, followed by the presentation of blackline masters.

Role of Caring

The impact of teachers on student learning is increased when students are taught by well-prepared professionals who combine their knowledge of the content and instruction with a deep sense of caring about their students. Effective teachers are not only caring (Johnson, 1997; Thomas & Montgomery, 1998), but also culturally competent and attuned to their students' interests and needs both in and out of school (Cruickshank & Haefele, 2001). This valuing of the student as an individual is important in establishing and sustaining relationships. Teachers who show that they care about students enhance the learning process and serve as role models to students (Collinson et al., 1999). Caring is expressed in many ways, including the following:

- ▲ listening,
- ▲ expressing feelings,
- ▲ knowing students on a personal level,
- ▲ demonstrating patience, honesty, trust, humility, hope, and courage,
- ▲ accommodating students' needs,
- ▲ using a considerate tone of voice and manner,
- ▲ paying attention to each student,
- ▲ showing receptive body language, and
- ▲ valuing students' input in problem solving (Collinson et al.; Deiro, 2003; Ford & Trotman, 2001; Thomas & Montgomery, 1998).

In a study of effective and ineffective teachers, researchers found that both groups of teachers were equally respectful of their students, but the effective teachers demonstrated better listening skills and the ability to express their feelings (Emmer, Evertson, & Anderson, 1980). Nearly 20 years later, another set of researchers found that adults reflecting on their most influential teachers highlighted the interpersonal attribute of caring as key to the effectiveness of those teachers (Peart & Campbell, 1999). Caring teachers create relationships where respect and learning are fostered so students feel safe taking risks that are associated with learning (Collinson et al., 1999). Caring is an important attribute of effective teachers, and students must be able to hear, see, and feel that caring in their daily contact with teachers.

Role of Fairness and Respect

Fairness and respect are two attributes that require ongoing effort to maintain. Situations constantly arise with students, colleagues, and others that test a teacher's commitment to these ideals. Obviously, everyone wants to be treated in a fair and respectful manner. Often, fairness and respect are embodied in class rules, thus demonstrating the importance of these concepts. Every action taken by a teacher in the classroom, especially involving discipline, can be perceived as fair or unfair. Perception is very powerful in determining fairness and respect, as each individual has his or her own internal definition of what constitutes such values. As a result, once student opinion has been set, it is difficult to change it. Particularly with elementary and middle school students, the idea of justice as explained in Lawrence Kohlberg's model of moral development* is very strong. Students want to see "right" triumph and be rewarded, while "wrongs" are punished.

Respect is a cornerstone of a classroom's foundation. Effective teachers demonstrate respect in a variety of ways, from their treatment of students to how they work with students' families. Equitable treatment of students, regardless of race, gender, and other differences, is vital (Peart & Campbell, 1999). Respectful teachers know their students by name early in the school year, value individual talents and abilities, are aware of students' moods, and respond to changes they observe (Burden & Byrd, 1994). Effective teachers also recognize that families are partners in students' education. Depending

---

*See educational psychology texts and other applicable sources for details regarding Kohlberg's theory of moral development. One source to consider is: Kohlberg, L. (1969). Stage and sequence: The cognitive-developmental approach to socialization. In D. Goslin (Ed.), *Handbook of socialization theory and research.* New York: Rand McNally.

on the families' desired level of involvement, the teacher responds in a variety of ways from simple communication to collaboration (Rockwell, Andre, & Hawley, 1996). In fact, effective teachers have been found to correspond more frequently with parents (Taylor, Pearson, Clark, & Walpole, 1999) using a variety of means, including telephone calls, notes, letters, home visits, e-mails, and school events (Collinson et al., 1999; Swap, 1993). By involving the students and their families, effective teachers are respecting the children's first teachers, their families, and engaging them as partners in the students' ongoing journey through school.

Attitude Toward the Teaching Profession

Teaching is a demanding profession, and yet effective teachers exude a sense of pride and accomplishment in their work. All teachers contribute to the profession through their words and actions. Those teachers and administrators who model high expectations for themselves tend to get the same from their students (Cawelti, 1999). Educators are constantly observed, not only in school, but also in the community, and what they say about the profession influences those who hear it. How teachers act affects people's impressions of teachers even more.

Teachers' attitudes about the profession most directly affect the school climate. Some teachers are collegial in their demeanor, while others are disengaged (Woolfolk-Hoy & Hoy, 2003). A collegial approach enhances the school climate and the learning environment for students, but a purely social or disengaged one does little to enhance student achievement. Teachers who are collegial serve their school through participation on committees, acting as mentors, supervising student teachers, supporting other teachers, and assuming leadership roles. When teachers interact with one another, they build a sense of community through the interactions. Positive outlooks create a healthy community that affects personal commitment, motivation, efficacy, and performance in the classroom (NWREL, 2001). A positive and productive school climate has the added benefits of infusing its members with increased satisfaction, enthusiasm, commitment, and empowerment as educators (Holloway, 2003). Effective teachers are realistic about the demands of their teaching assignments, but are dedicated to making a difference in the lives of students.

Social Interactions with Students

Social interactions between teachers and students play a significant role in cultivating a positive learning environment, both within the classroom and in the school as a whole. These interactions are a natural outgrowth of caring by the teacher and are based on a genuine interest in students and a concern for their welfare (Ford & Trotman, 2001; Noddings, 1992; Peart & Campbell, 1999). Positive social interactions are fostered through meaningful dialogue, common areas of interest, and shared experiences that can take place during class, at lunch, or during extracurricular activities. "Teachers need to allow students to see them as complete people with emotions, opinions, and lives outside of school" (Wolk, 2003, p. 18). When teachers interact with students in a warm, personal manner, students feel affirmed as people and learners, thereby enhancing achievement (Thomas & Montgomery, 1998). Strong teacher-student relationships also reduce discipline problems (Wolk, 2002).

Effective teachers establish a dynamic relationship with students that evolves as students' needs change and as each party becomes better acquainted with the other. These teachers are friendly, understanding, and confident (Wubbels et al., 1997). The personal connection that they make with students assists in creating a trusting and respectful relationship (Marzano, Pickering, & McTighe, 1993; McBer, 2000) that becomes a building block for pushing students to new heights. "Trust is likely to be sustained as people interact in cooperative ways" (Tschannen-Moran & Hoy, 2000, p. 574). Effective teachers convey a sense that students are valued and that they enjoy working with students (Haberman, 1995). In turn, students work harder for teachers who they perceive as being honest with them and who believe in their abilities (Haberman). The relationship becomes a source of influence that is fueled by the interpersonal dynamic between teacher and student (NWREL, 2001). In the converse, when students do not perceive trust, they do not learn as well (Tschannen-Moran & Hoy). As noted by Ted Sizer, "we cannot teach students well if we do not know them well" (1999, p. 6).

Promotion of Enthusiasm and Motivation for Learning

Teachers fulfill multiple roles in their classrooms. They provide support to students in a variety of ways that result in increased student achievement and confidence (NWREL, 2001). To use a sports analogy, teachers are coaches, athletic trainers, equipment managers, and cheerleaders all rolled into one. In each of these roles, teachers convey enthusiasm and a motivation to excel for their players. As a coach, the teacher has a game plan for learning and explains it in precise detail to ensure that students are capable of successfully executing it. As the athletic trainer, the teacher assumes the role of patching up players so that they are not hampered by previous injuries. As the equipment manager, the teacher ensures that students have the resources they need to get the job done. Finally, as the cheerleader, the teacher eventually moves to the sidelines as the players are ready to execute a game plan on their own with the support they need. In sports, the coach is often hailed if the team is doing well and pummeled if performance is poor. Effective teachers are most like coaches in that it is their responsibility to see that students are successful in learning (Corbett, Wilson, & Williams, 2002; Ford & Trotman, 2001).

Effective educators use their own enthusiasm for the subject as a tool to reach and motivate students. They are enthusiastic about the content they are teaching (Peart & Campbell, 1999) and they convey this feeling to their students through the activities they select, the energy they project, and their competence in the subject area. Effective teachers recognize that motivation is critical to fostering and enhancing learning in students (NWREL, 2001). Their goal is not simply to present the material, but to see students succeed in acquiring new knowledge (Ford & Trotman, 2001). In order to do this, effective teachers use a variety of strategies such as student goal setting, choice in assignments, cooperative learning, self-paced instruction, and self-assessment (Fisher, 2003). Think back to movies such as *Stand and Deliver*, *Mr. Holland's Opus*, and *Dangerous Minds*. All of these movies portrayed teachers who believed in their students and offered them guidance and affirmation when they were unsure of themselves. Effective teachers actively engage students in learning and foster a genuine motivation to learn. They tap into students' natural curiosity and draw extraordinary results from them.

Role of Reflective Practice

People refer to hindsight as being 20/20. For effective teachers, this nod to hindsight is more than a casual observation or startling insight—it is a deliberate and thoughtful reflection that is a part of professional practice. "Reflection is the 'supervisor' that encourages teachers to continue what worked and correct what isn't working" (Harris, 2003, p. 39). It is an internal monitoring system that teachers use to process the multitude of external stimuli they experience on a daily basis. Reflection is about learning from experience.

Many educators are introduced to reflection during their preservice teaching program, but reflection is not limited to novices in the profession. For effective teachers, it is a lifelong professional practice (Grossman et al., 2000; Thomas & Montgomery, 1998). Teachers must know themselves and their goals to reflect upon their progress toward meeting them. Reflection can also be used to create an alignment between what teachers believe and how they behave (Corcoran & Leahy, 2003). Reflection is not an easy undertaking, as teachers must be open to confronting the fact that there is much that they do not know and cannot anticipate (Thomas & Montomery). Fortunately, teachers do not have to enter into reflection in isolation; they can get feedback and assistance from a variety of sources.

Reflection may be driven by questions, research, new experiences, observations made on lesson plans, journals, and discussion with colleagues. One approach suggests thinking of a critical incident and then describing the problem, players, possible solutions, chosen plan of action, rationale for the action, and outcomes (Harris, 2003). Preservice teachers are taught how to analyze and reflect on their practice and what they observe others doing (Burden & Byrd, 1994). In a study that followed 10 preservice teachers through student teaching and into their first two years of classroom teaching, researchers found that students "heard" the voices of their education professors as part of their reflection when dealing with a dilemma and, in fact, were able to apply some of what they learned in their preparation programs during the second year that eluded them during the first "survival" year (Grossman, et al., 2000). No matter how teachers choose to do it, reflection is a very personal and introspective analysis of their professional lives, and is an essential practice for good teachers.

Visualizing the Quality

What we are hoping to capture in this flow chart (Figure 2.2) is that some quality indicators are best considered as input variables for describing the teacher as a person (caring, fairness and respect, and attitude); others are best considered as output variables (promotion of enthusiasm, motivation for learning, and social interactions with students). Reflection might be considered as an overarching attitude and behavior that supports and enhances all personal attributes. It is important to note, however, that all of these quality indicators—whether characterized as input or output variables—ultimately define the personality and behavior of the teacher.

FIGURE 2.2

Visual Representation of Teacher as a Person

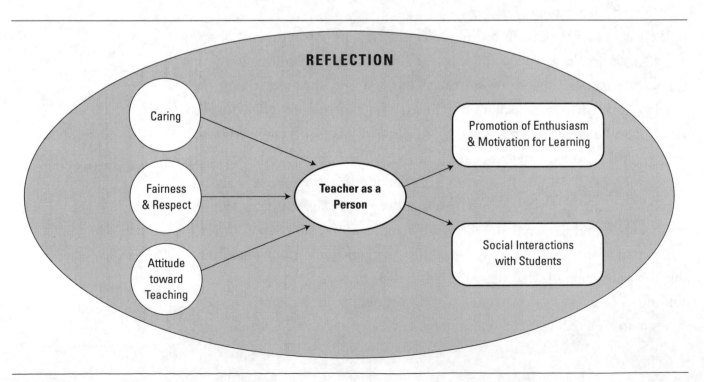

Focus on the Teacher

Barbara Wells is struggling to adjust to her new surroundings. She knows she is a good teacher, but she just needs to figure out what makes this group of students tick. Barbara sometimes feels like she and her students are doing well, but she wants more than a cordial relationship with them; she wants real rapport with her students. She misses the relationships she had with her students in her previous school.

The Teacher as a Person:
Self-Assessing Key Quality Indicators

Barbara used Figure 2.3 to identify areas where she could improve. She knew that she had made adjustments in her instructional delivery upon coming to the new school and that her fellow colleagues were right about her classroom's uncomfortable tone. Barbara just could not put her finger on what was different in the way she worked with students. She knew that she valued them and worked hard to meet their needs, but she still was not connecting with her students in the way she had with previous classes that she had taught.

The Teacher as a Person:
Building Bridges to Resolve Dilemmas

One tool that Barbara can use to brainstorm ways to increase her interactions with students is found in Figure 2.4. This form is a visual way to see a means of getting from the current situation to the desired situation.

Caring, Fairness, and Respect:
Gauging Student Opinion

Barbara has established a very business-like classroom where the work generally gets done and learning occurs. She does not have a strong sense of what the students really think of one another or of her, as Barbara tends to control interactions. One activity she can do with her students is making bookmarks that provide students with an opportunity to say what strengths

FIGURE 2.3

Assessing Qualities Associated with
The Teacher as a Person

Directions: Circle the number that best describes the degree to which you do each item, then use page two to analyze the responses.

**Reflect on the Teacher:
Case 2A**

• *Identify Barbara's strengths and weaknesses in terms of personal qualities.*

• *How does her relative weakness in the "Interactions with Students" quality indicator affect her teaching?*

		Rarely	Occasion-ally	Usually	Almost Always
1.	I am responsible for student success.	1	2	③	4
2.	I understand my students.	1	②	3	4
3.	I communicate with my students' families at least monthly.	①	2	3	4
4.	I admit my mistakes.	1	2	③	4
5.	I dress like a professional teacher.	1	2	3	④
6.	I maintain student confidentiality.	1	2	3	④
7.	I am responsive to my students' needs.	1	2	③	4
8.	I spend time with my students outside of assigned class time.	①	2	3	4
9.	I enjoy teaching.	1	2	3	④
10.	I like teaching my content/subject/grade level.	1	2	3	④
11.	I listen attentively to student questions and comments.	1	2	3	④
12.	I treat others with respect, even in difficult situations.	1	2	3	④
13.	I get to know all my students as individuals.	1	②	3	4
14.	I speak in an appropriate tone to others.	1	2	3	④
15.	I know all my students by name the first week of school.	1	②	3	4
16.	I attend activities in which my students are participating that are not related to my class.	1	②	3	4
17.	I know my students outside of school.	①	2	3	4
18.	I reflect on dilemmas I encounter in the classroom.	1	2	③	4
19.	I learn from my past experiences in the classroom.	1	2	③	4
20.	I want to see my students succeed.	1	2	3	④
21.	I feel that I am an important part of the school community.	1	②	3	4
22.	I am satisfied with the balance between my professional and personal life.	1	2	③	4
23.	I accept responsibility for decisions I make in the classroom.	1	2	3	④
24.	I use strategies to engage my students as learners.	1	2	③	4

FIGURE 2.3

Assessing Qualities Associated with
The Teacher as a Person (continued)

Directions: Transfer the number that was circled for each question to the corresponding spaces provided below. After transferring all the numbers, add them by the category and calculate the average. Finally, color the bar graph cells to show the average in each key quality indicator.

	Caring		**Fairness & Respect**		**Teaching Attitude**
2.	2	3.	1	5.	4
7.	3	6.	4	9.	4
11.	4	12.	4	21.	2
15.	2	14.	4	22.	3
Total	11	**Total**	13	**Total**	13
Average = Total/4	2.75	**Average = Total/4**	3.25	**Average = Total/4**	3.25

	Interactions with Students		**Enthusiasm & Motivation**		**Reflective Practice**
8.	1	1.	3	4.	3
13.	2	10.	4	18.	3
16.	2	20.	4	19.	3
17.	1	24.	3	23.	4
Total	6	**Total**	14	**Total**	13
Average = Total/4	1.5	**Average = Total/4**	3.5	**Average = Total/4**	3.25

Profile of the Teacher as a Person Key Quality Indicators

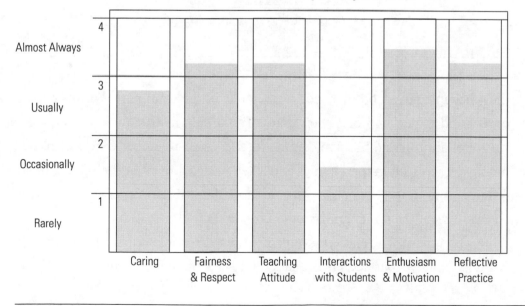

➤

**Reflect on the Teacher:
Case 2B**

*All teachers who are new to
the school system but have
prior teaching experience are
assigned a school-based
contact. This person has different responsibilities than a
mentor for a novice teacher.
Barbara shared her bridge
diagram with her contact. If
you were the contact, what
additional strategies would
you suggest to Barbara to
help her connect with the
inner-city youth in this high-
poverty school?*

FIGURE 2.4
Building Bridges

This visual provides a method for thinking about the starting point, what the desired outcome is, and the challenges that must be addressed.

Directions: Place the situation on the left of the page and the desired outcome on the right. Identify challenges by placing them in the water under the bridge. On the bridge, list strategies to assist in achieving the desired outcome.

Strategies
- Have students write their autobiographies as the topic for the 7th grade research paper . . . they could include interviews, etc.
- Do an interest inventory to see what students like
- Have a highlights board in the room where students can share accomplishments/announcements
- Use homeroom time to talk with students . . . maybe organize a talk show format to get kids discussing topics they are interested in
- Try to stay after school one day every week to help students OR watch an after-school sporting/band/drama event
- Invite students to have lunch chats with me in small groups

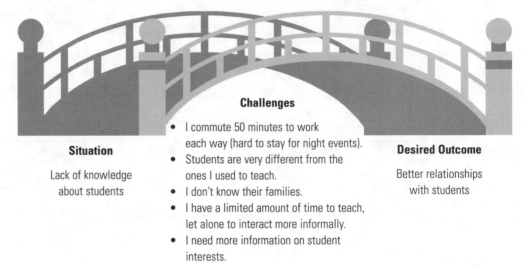

Challenges
- I commute 50 minutes to work each way (hard to stay for night events).
- Students are very different from the ones I used to teach.
- I don't know their families.
- I have a limited amount of time to teach, let alone to interact more informally.
- I need more information on student interests.

Situation

Lack of knowledge about students

Desired Outcome

Better relationships with students

they recognize in each other. The teacher fills in the team name, prints copies on colored paper, and cuts them into strips. Class instructions focus on the nature of appropriate positive comments and emphasize that they are anonymous. Students fill in their names and leave the bookmark at their seats. In an orderly fashion (it often helps to say no more than two students at a desk with a bookmark at the same time), students go to their classmates' bookmarks and write a comment. The teacher is a member of the team and is included as well. Figure 2.5 shows Barbara's bookmark after students filled it out.

FIGURE 2.5

Bookmark that Barbara Wells's Students Filled in About Her

The _____ Dolphin _____
Team Values the Strengths of
Mrs. Wells

*Those strengths are the following as
seen by fellow teammates.*

Niceness
Creativity
Cool teacher
Nice teacher all around
Creative
Nice & Funny
Always here
Spiffy in the Jiffy way
Cool teacher
What they said
Sneaker lady
Knows a lot
Lots of story ideas
Your aunt has a carpet rake
Nice
Spiffy in the Jif way
Good teacher
Tries hard
Nice
Likes cats
Smart
Nice
Nice
Perfect attendance
Neat
Nice shoes

◀

**Reflect on the Teacher:
Case 2C**

- *What do Barbara's students think about her?*

- *What on the bookmark may have surprised Barbara?*

  – *Why would students perceive these items as strengths?*

  – *How can she use the students' opinions to improve?*

Increasing Social Interactions with Students

Erica Beckham, the English lead teacher, observed Barbara teaching a lesson on the book *Tuck Everlasting*. She knew Barbara was struggling to connect with her students and was interested in seeing how they interacted in class. Figure 2.6 is an instrument based on Flander's Interaction Analysis Methodology (1985), and is designed to capture actual teacher behaviors at regular intervals as the teacher interacts with students.

➤

**Reflect on the Teacher:
Case 2D**

- *From looking at the 1.5-hour snapshot of Barbara's lesson, what do you* know *about her interactions with students, what can be* inferred *about her relationship with the class, and* what questions *do you have about the lesson?*

- *How can this observational analysis help Barbara reflect?*

FIGURE 2.6

Interaction During a Lesson on Tuck Everlasting

Student-Teacher Interaction Chart

Observer: Erica Beckham   **Date:** 11/19

Teacher: Barbara Wells   **Start & End Times:** 8–9:30 am

Grade/Subjects: English, Grade 7

School: Happy Hollow Middle School

Tally the number of times each interactive behavior occurs during your observation period. Try to record at least one example or quote of each type of interaction. At the end of the observation period, total the number of all teacher-student interactions and calculate the percentage of the total for each interaction.

	Type of Interactive Behavior	Tally of Times Observed	Percentage
INDIRECT	Accepts Feelings *Example:* Made a solemn face and nodded	//	1.5%
	Praises/Encourages *Example:* "Good response, go pick out a dividend" (these are colorful easers and pencils in a box)	///	2.3%
	Accepts or Uses Student Ideas *Example:* "Yes, that is a good point"	### ///	6.8%
	Asks Questions *Example:* "Why would a parent choose to let their child drink from the spring?"	### ### ### ### ### ### ###	26.5%

FIGURE 2.6
Interaction During a Lesson
on <u>Tuck Everlasting</u> (continued)

Student-Teacher Interaction

	Type of Interactive Behavior	Tally of Times Observed	Percentage
DIRECT	Gives Information (lectures) *Example:* Mini-lectures (e.g., reviews vocabulary, previous events)	////	3.0%
	Gives Directions *Example:* "Turn to your partner and share what you read last night, then talk about what you think about what just occurred"	### ### ### ### ### ### ### //	28.0%
	Corrects without Rejection *Example:* "Remember in the story how Jesse and Winnie met . . . "	### //	6.8%
	Criticizes Student Response *Example:* "Now (student's name), you know you can do better than that"	//	1.5%
	Reprimands or Asserts Authority *Example:* "(students' names) you should not be talking about band, right now."	///	2.3%
STUDENT TALK	Student Talk Response: Individual *Example:* "The stranger wanted to sell the spring water"	### ### ### ### /	16.5%
	Student Talk Response: Choral "Winnie"; "Yes"; "No"; etc.	###	3.9%
	Student Talk Initiation *Example:* Buzz about if the stranger had a right to sell the spring water or if it would be stealing.	////	3.0%
TOTALS		132	102.1*

*overage due to rounding
The type of interaction most frequently used: Giving directions and asking questions

Guided Reflective Practice

Earlier in this chapter, Barbara's self-assessment (Figure 2.3) indicated that she regularly reflects on her practice, but we don't know how she does so or what this means to her. It is quite possible that she reflects on her day during her commute home or in a journal each night. Figure 2.7 is a format that can be used for guided reflection. It encourages the teacher to look at a dilemma from different angles and evaluate the course of action.

FIGURE 2.7
Reflection Dialogue Journal Entry

Dilemma

LaToya came in today without her homework again (it was the seventh time this month). I did not even ask her why, I just gave her a note to have her mother sign and requested the work be brought to me the next day. It works about half the time. . . follow-up phone calls are used when necessary. She became very agitated . . . it took five minutes of class time to calm her down.

When Alonzo did not have his work (first time this year), I did ask him why and he told me that he had to go with his father to the emergency room and watch his little brother while his sister was seen for her high fever. He said he did not get home until 1 a.m. I conveyed my concern for his sister and told him to just bring me the work the next day .

What did I perceive?

LaToya repeatedly does not have her work and this was a first-time issue for Alonzo. I thought I was being compassionate about his circumstances and not dwelling on LaToya's lack of work.

What were the alternative viewpoints?

LaToya was angry; she said that I wasn't being fair and that she, too, had a reason for not doing her homework. She had been at a funeral for a relative of her mother's boyfriend and had gotten home around 10 p.m.

LaToya called Alonzo the teacher's pet and other students started making "bow wow" noises.

What did I choose to do?

I started the class on the assignment (although most did not appear to be doing their work, seeming to listen into my conversation with LaToya). I pulled LaToya aside and asked her what was wrong (got the story) and then told her that I would like to talk to her more after class and would give her a note to her math class. She and I met later and she seemed to be okay. She nodded that she understood why I was "easier" on Alonzo than her. LaToya told me that I embarrassed her when I just gave her the note to get signed.

What else could I have done?

- Asked students who did not have homework to see me after class . . . or after the class started their independent practice
- Could have sent the two students to my teammate's class while we went over the homework
- Publicly announced at the start of the school year that everyone gets a "no questions asked" pass each semester if they need to turn in homework a day late
- Not been so defensive when LaToya started fussing…my reaction probably made it worse
- Addressed the issue of respect . . . I wanted to get the other students started with something else, but I left Alonzo to be the subject of disrespect

What additional actions should I take as a follow-up?

Call LaToya's mother and make sure she is okay because she seemed rather upset in class . . . also have a class discussion on respect using the framework of how do we get it, how do we show it, how do we keep it. Also, I should continue to insist that students, including LaToya, keep up with homework. After all, unless they succeed, my compassion likely will not help them that much down the road.

Reflect on the Teacher: Case 2E

- As an outsider looking at this situation, what additional insights can you add?

- What advantages (or disadvantages) are there to recording dilemmas using the form?

Making Connections

Consider the Scenario

Reread the teacher scenario at the beginning of this chapter and the bits of information shared on the sample forms about Barbara. Consider the questions below.

Using the space below, brainstorm about what positive attributes exist and what performance areas need improvement for Barbara.

Positive Attributes	Areas for Improvement

What descriptor best describes Barbara's skills in the area of "teacher as a person"?

_____ Master: demonstrates the complexity of the quality resulting in a rich learning experience for students

_____ Professional: demonstrates the quality most of the time so there is a productive learning experience for students

_____ Apprentice: demonstrates the quality well enough for learning to occur, but performance is inconsistent

_____ Undeveloped: demonstrates sub-par performance of the quality

Why did you select a particular descriptor?

How could Barbara's performance be improved?

Reflecting on My Current Performance

Rate your performance on the qualities associated with the teacher as a person using the explanation of each descriptor from the previous page.

	Undeveloped	Apprentice	Professional	Master
Caring				
Fairness and Respect				
Attitude Toward Teaching				
Interactions with Students				
Enthusiasm and Motivation				
Reflective Practice				

Reflection Learning Log

What do I better understand now after studying and reflecting upon the quality of the teacher as a person?

What are next steps to improve my performance?

What resources (e.g., people and materials) are needed to enhance my teaching effectiveness?

Resources

This section contains two items: 1) the *Authors' Perspective* and 2) *blackline masters* of forms that can be used to promote improvement and reflection on qualities of effective teachers.

Reflect on the Teacher: Authors' Perspective

The Reflect on the Teacher questions are provided throughout the chapter to encourage interaction with the book. In most cases, there are no precisely right or wrong answers. The *Authors' Perspective* is provided as one way to reflect on the information presented.

Reflect on the Teacher: Case 2A (see p. 40)

Identify Barbara's strengths and weaknesses.

Strengths: Barbara's scores on Fairness & Respect, Enthusiasm & Motivation, Reflective Practice, and Teaching Attitude indicate that Barbara felt that she demonstrated those behaviors often.

Weakness: Interactions with students.

How does her weakness affect her teaching?

Barbara perceives herself to be a high performer in many of the key quality indicator areas. The interactions with students category refers to her relationships with students outside of the assigned classroom time. Looking at just the assessment, one could infer that she does not spend time getting to know her students in settings other than class. When teachers develop a relationship with their students outside of the classroom, they often have fewer disciplinary issues (Thomas & Montgomery, 1998). It also is easier to establish rapport with students and make them feel valued as individuals (Peart & Campbell, 1999). Barbara probably feels like the technical aspects of teaching are fine, but the interpersonal components of her practice are relatively weaker.

Reflect on the Teacher: Case 2B (see p. 42)

All teachers who are new to the school system but have prior teaching experience are assigned a school-based contact. This person has different responsibilities than a mentor for a novice teacher. Barbara shared her bridge diagram with her contact. If you were the contact, what additional strategies would you suggest to Barbara to help her connect with the inner-city youth in this high-poverty school?

Barbara identified several strategies that she could implement. She might also consider the following activities:

▲ Getting to know where the students live. She could do this by riding along on an afternoon bus route.

▲ Attending as many evening events as possible at the school to get to know some of the families of her students.

▲ Attending sporting events in the community to see her students outside of class.

▲ Reading the local newspaper to find out what is going on in the students' community. Because Barbara lives about 50 minutes away from the school, reading the local news can help keep her in touch. In particular, she should focus on the local news section.

▲ Making positive phone calls or sending notes home recognizing the good work students are doing will increase her rapport with them. They will appreciate her noticing what they are doing well. A goal of just two per week would result in over 72 good contacts in a year, and four contacts a week would allow her to make a positive contact with all her students at least once.

▲ Attending training offered by the school system on cultural competence. Learning how to build additional relationships with families and the community. In this school, these two elements are particularly important.

Reflect on the Teacher: Case 2C (see p. 43)

What do Barbara's students think about her?

The most common adjective used was *nice*; while this is a rather generic descriptor, it does convey an overall positive opinion of Barbara as a person. They recognized that she knew her content area and was creative. In general, they think she is a good teacher.

What on the bookmark may have surprised Barbara?

She may have been surprised by the observations about her shoes (worn due to foot problems), the mention of her attendance record, and the fact they remembered her cat and the story about her aunt.

Why would students perceive these items as strengths?

The shoes could be an indication of the discontinuity the students perceive between Barbara's professional dress and her choice of footwear. They may find this novel, or it could be a veiled jab. The recalling of specific stories shows that Barbara was able to engage and connect with students in such a way that they remembered personal information. The attendance record is probably the most telling. The students who noticed that Barbara had not missed a day of school were sending a message that it matters to them that she is there every day for them. They like her dependability.

How can she use the students' opinions to improve?

Barbara should be reassured that the students value what she has to offer and feel more secure in sharing herself with them. By calling Barbara nice, students indicated their perception of her being fair, respectful, and caring. In the absence of any comments about her ability to generate enthusiasm and motivation or her social interactions with students, she might want to work on conveying these qualities to students.

Reflect on the Teacher: Case 2D (see p. 44)

From looking at the 1.5-hour snapshot of Barbara's lesson (Figure 2.6), what do you know about her interactions with students, what can be inferred about her relationship with the class, and what questions do you have about the lesson?

▲ *Know:* This was a very teacher-centered lesson. Barbara controlled most of the talking and interaction that occurred and the students did not bring up many of their own thoughts. There were more questions asked by Barbara (35) than there were responses by individual students (21) or the group as a whole (5). Barbara only praised students or used their ideas in the discussion 12 times.

▲ *Infer:* Based on how few questions were asked by students, they did not seem to be very engaged in the book—or, at least, the lesson about the book. They may not have read the assignment or they may be too uncomfortable to ask questions in the large class setting. Barbara spends a lot of time giving directions, which could be alleviated by developing classroom routines with students. (*Please see Chapter 4 for additional details on establishing classroom routines and organizing for instruction.*)

▲ *Questions:* How long have the students been working on this book? Could the students be bored with the book? Does Barbara sometimes let the students lead the discussions? Where did the questions Barbara asked come from? Why doesn't Barbara affirm some students more often? Given the discrepancy between the number of questions asked and responses, is she providing sufficient wait time? What is Barbara's perception of how she interacts with students in class?

How can this observational analysis help Barbara reflect?

If Erica showed Barbara a blank copy of the Student-Teacher Interaction Chart and asked her to rank the interactions from 1–12, with 1 being the interaction she had the most often with students, Barbara would be able to compare her perceptions with the data collected. Barbara may not realize the degree to which she is spending time asking questions and giving directions as opposed to really offering praise, feedback, and support to students. It may be that only a subtle shift in instructional strategies and feedback to students would result in a more personalized and engaging lesson.

Reflect on the Teacher: Case 2E (see p. 47)

As an outsider looking at this situation, what additional insights can you add?

The respect component and not losing face in front of peers is very important. LaToya's actions were not about humiliating Alonzo; rather, they were her defense mechanism to deflect attention away from herself. The importance placed on the event must be strong if LaToya's mother felt it was important enough to take her daughter to the funeral of a boyfriend's cousin. Barbara could follow-up with the mother to find out if LaToya needs any additional support. From the information given, one does not know what LaToya's relationship was with the cousin . . . he or she may have been someone her age, a person she saw at family events, or a family acquaintance. The teasing directed toward Alonzo was not addressed. Barbara needed to make it clear that teasing was not permitted in her class. She could have used the incident as a teachable moment to assert that respect is fundamental to creating a safe learning environment in the classroom.

What advantages (or disadvantages) are there to recording dilemmas using the form?

A disadvantage is that the process can be time consuming. Perhaps it could be reserved for either especially challenging situations or for periodic, randomly selected class events. One advantage of the process is that writing down the situation can be cathartic and can help teachers process their own feelings and perceptions about the situation. In addition, using the form can help a teacher objectively identify and examine the issues associated with the dilemma. The form also can be placed in a file so that the teacher can document reflections over time and compare experiences if a similar situation arises again.

Blackline Masters

The following blackline masters can be photocopied and used in your school or district.

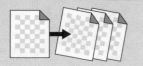

Assessing Qualities Associated with **The Teacher as a Person**

Directions: Circle the number that best describes the degree to which you do each item, then use page two to analyze the responses.

	Rarely	Occasion-ally	Usually	Almost Always
1. I am responsible for student success.	1	2	3	4
2. I understand my students.	1	2	3	4
3. I communicate with my students' families at least monthly.	1	2	3	4
4. I admit my mistakes.	1	2	3	4
5. I dress like a professional teacher.	1	2	3	4
6. I maintain student confidentiality.	1	2	3	4
7. I am responsive to my students' needs.	1	2	3	4
8. I spend time with my students outside of assigned class time.	1	2	3	4
9. I enjoy teaching.	1	2	3	4
10. I like teaching my content/subject/grade level.	1	2	3	4
11. I listen attentively to student questions and comments.	1	2	3	4
12. I treat others with respect, even in difficult situations.	1	2	3	4
13. I get to know all my students as individuals.	1	2	3	4
14. I speak in an appropriate tone to others.	1	2	3	4
15. I know all my students by name the first week of school.	1	2	3	4
16. I attend activities in which my students are participating that are not related to my class.	1	2	3	4
17. I know my students outside of school.	1	2	3	4
18. I reflect on dilemmas I encounter in the classroom.	1	2	3	4
19. I learn from my past experiences in the classroom.	1	2	3	4
20. I want to see my students succeed.	1	2	3	4
21. I feel that I am an important part of the school community.	1	2	3	4
22. I am satisfied with the balance between my professional and personal life.	1	2	3	4
23. I accept responsibility for decisions I make in the classroom.	1	2	3	4
24. I use strategies to engage my students as learners.	1	2	3	4

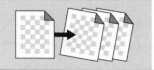

Assessing Qualities Associated with <u>The Teacher as a Person</u> (continued)

Directions: Transfer the number that was circled for each question to the corresponding spaces provided below. After transferring all the numbers, add them by the category and calculate the average. Finally, color in the bar graph cells to show the average in each key quality indicator.

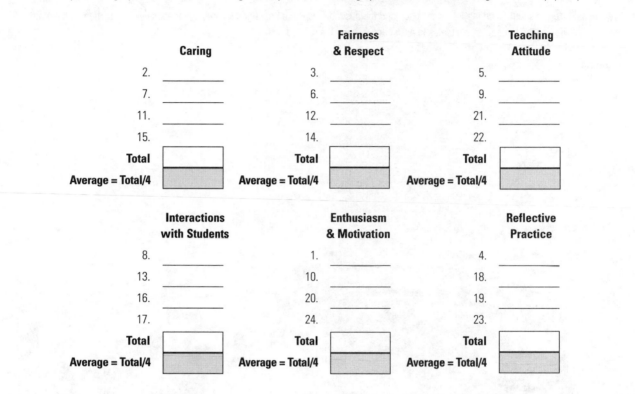

Caring

2. _____
7. _____
11. _____
15. _____
Total ⬜
Average = Total/4 ▨

Fairness & Respect

3. _____
6. _____
12. _____
14. _____
Total ⬜
Average = Total/4 ▨

Teaching Attitude

5. _____
9. _____
21. _____
22. _____
Total ⬜
Average = Total/4 ▨

Interactions with Students

8. _____
13. _____
16. _____
17. _____
Total ⬜
Average = Total/4 ▨

Enthusiasm & Motivation

1. _____
10. _____
20. _____
24. _____
Total ⬜
Average = Total/4 ▨

Reflective Practice

4. _____
18. _____
19. _____
23. _____
Total ⬜
Average = Total/4 ▨

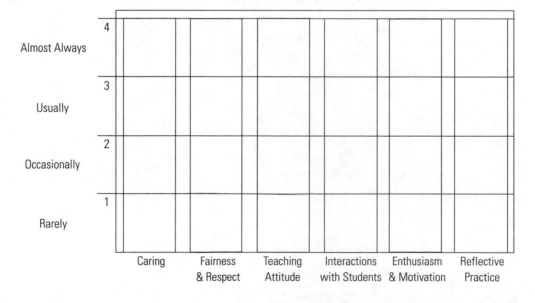

Profile of the Teacher as a Person Key Quality Indicators

	Caring	Fairness & Respect	Teaching Attitude	Interactions with Students	Enthusiasm & Motivation	Reflective Practice
4 Almost Always						
3 Usually						
2 Occasionally						
1 Rarely						

Building Bridges

This visual provides a method for thinking about the starting point, what the desired outcome is, and the challenges that must be addressed.

Directions: Place the situation on the left of the page and the desired outcome on the right. Identify challenges by placing them in the water under the bridge. On the bridge, list strategies to assist in achieving the desired outcome.

Strategies

Challenges

Situation

Desired Outcome

Bookmarks

The _____
Team Values the Strengths of
_____

Those strengths are the following as seen by fellow teammates.

_____
_____
_____
_____
_____
_____
_____
_____
_____
_____
_____
_____
_____
_____
_____
_____
_____
_____
_____
_____
_____
_____
_____
_____
_____
_____
_____

The _____
Team Values the Strengths of
_____

Those strengths are the following as seen by fellow teammates.

_____
_____
_____
_____
_____
_____
_____
_____
_____
_____
_____
_____
_____
_____
_____
_____
_____
_____
_____
_____
_____
_____
_____
_____
_____
_____
_____

The _____
Team Values the Strengths of
_____

Those strengths are the following as seen by fellow teammates.

_____
_____
_____
_____
_____
_____
_____
_____
_____
_____
_____
_____
_____
_____
_____
_____
_____
_____
_____
_____
_____
_____
_____
_____
_____
_____
_____

Student-Teacher Interaction Chart

Observer: _____ **Date:** _____

Teacher: _____ **Start & End Times:** _____

Grade/Subjects: _____

School: _____

Tally the number of times each interactive behavior occurs during your observation period. Try to record at least one example or quote of each type of interaction. At the end of the observation period, total the number of all teacher-student interactions and calculate the percentage of the total for each interaction.

Type of Interactive Behavior		Tally of Times Observed	Percentage
INDIRECT	Accepts Feelings *Example:*		
	Praises/Encourages *Example:*		
	Accepts or Uses Student Ideas *Example:*		
	Asks Questions *Example:*		

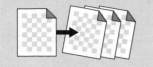

Student-Teacher Interaction Chart (continued)

	Type of Interactive Behavior	Tally of Times Observed	Percentage
DIRECT	Gives Information (lectures) *Example:*		
	Gives Directions *Example:*		
	Corrects without Rejection *Example:*		
	Criticizes Student Response *Example:*		
	Reprimands or Asserts Authority *Example:*		
STUDENT TALK	Student Talk Response: Individual *Example:*		
	Student Talk Response: Choral *Example:*		
	Student Talk Initiation *Example:*		

TOTALS

The type of interaction most frequently used:

Reflection Dialogue Journal Entry

Dilemma

What did I perceive?

What were the alternative viewpoints?

What did I choose to do?

What else could I have done?

What additional actions should I take as a follow-up?

CLASSROOM MANAGEMENT AND ORGANIZATION

As a second-year teacher, Mandrel Epps is showing a lot of promise, but he still has some rough edges. He works very hard to develop engaging lessons and accompanying materials. Another teacher on his grade level said that if she shares an activity with him, he gives it back with some additional, and often better, twists. Mandrel showed a lot of courage coming back to teach after the tough first year when he had 12 of the most challenging students in the grade level placed in his classroom. Mandrel's students say they like him and he makes learning interesting, but sometimes they also take advantage of him. It is as if he has a jigsaw box of puzzle pieces, but he cannot get all the pieces to fit together. He just doesn't seem to understand how to manage a classroom.

Research Summary

The classroom is a vehicle for getting students from where they are when they enter the schoolhouse door to where they need to be an academic year later. Ideally, we all would like to see at least one year of progress for one year of seat time. In talking about classroom management and student achievement, it may help to think of the teacher as the driver of the car who needs to respond to the passengers' needs in order to ensure that they reach their destination. In driver education there is a substantial focus on the mechanics of driving and the rules of the road, but not very much attention is given to keeping the automobile functioning. People learn about preventative maintenance as a secondary set of skills through guidance, observation, reading, and trial and error. The first flat tire or dead battery becomes a significant learning experience. Great driving skills don't matter when the car won't move. Similarly, great instructional skills won't matter if students in the classroom are disengaged or out of control. Both novice and experienced teachers consider classroom management to be a high priority and an area of concern (Sokal, Smith, & Mowat, 2003). Teachers learn "tricks of the trade" from such sources as watching other teachers, reading about the topic, and reflecting on what is occurring in their classrooms. While mastering effective classroom management techniques takes work, effective teachers make classroom management look easy. When an effective teacher is in the driver's seat, one knows that a preventative, proactive, positive approach is in place to ensure that learning is on course.

The classroom environment is influenced by the guidelines established for its operation, its users, and its physical elements. Teachers often have little control over issues such as temperature and leaky ceilings, but they greatly influence the operation of their classrooms. Effective teachers expertly manage and organize the classroom and expect their students to contribute in a positive and productive manner. It seems prudent to pay careful attention to classroom climate, given that it can have as much impact on student learning as student aptitude (Wang, Haertel, & Walberg, 1993). Effective teachers take time in the beginning of the year and especially on the first day of school (Emmer, Evertson, & Anderson, 1980; Emmer, Evertson, & Worsham, 2003) to establish classroom management, classroom organization, and expectations for student behavior.

▲ *Classroom Management* is "the actions and strategies teachers use to solve the problem of order in classrooms" (Doyle, 1986, p. 397). Effective teachers also use rules, procedures, and routines to ensure that students are actively involved in learning (Marzano, Marzano, & Pickering, 2003). In essence, they use management not to control student behavior, but to influence and direct it in a constructive manner to set the stage for instruction (McLeod, Fisher, & Hoover, 2003).

▲ *Classroom Organization* focuses on the physical environment. Effective teachers organize a safe classroom environment (Educational

Review Office, 1998). They strategically place furniture, learning centers, and materials in order to optimize student learning and reduce distractions.

▲ **Expectations for Student Behavior** is a key element in setting expectations for students. (Note: A second key, *Expectations for Achievement,* is discussed in Chapter 4 of the *Handbook.*) Effective teachers know that student behavior is not only about rules and consequences (McLeod et al., 2003); they also know that a larger component is the development of a classroom climate that influences how students perceive their environment and behave (Woolfolk-Hoy & Hoy, 2003). Thus, effective teachers expect students to act in a manner that contributes to a positive classroom environment.

This sampling of findings highlights the complexity of teaching as it relates to classroom management. Figure 3.1 provides a visual overview of this chapter. Following an elaboration of the three key quality indicators associated with the quality of classroom management and organization, tools to enhance effectiveness are presented in the context of our fictional teacher,

FIGURE 3.1

Chapter Overview

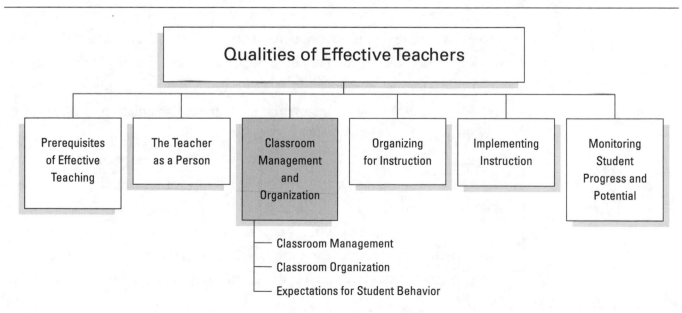

Mandrel. The questions posed in the *Focus on the Teacher* section are addressed at the end of the chapter before the presentation of the blackline masters.

Classroom Management

Effective teachers create focused and nurturing classrooms that result in increased student learning (Marzano et al., 2003; Shellard & Protheroe, 2000). These teachers teach and rehearse rules and procedures with students, anticipate students' needs, possess a plan to orient new students, and offer clear instructions to students (McLeod et al., 2003; Emmer et al., 1980). They use a minimum number of rules to ensure safety and productive interaction in the classroom, and they rely on routines to maintain a smoothly running classroom (McLeod et al. 2003). In fact, it has been noted that classroom management skills are essential in a classroom for a teacher to get anything done (Brophy & Evertson, 1976). In some ways, classroom management is like salt in a recipe; when it is present it is not noticed, but when it is missing, diners will ask for it.

Rules

Virtually everything that involves interactions among people requires rules. Webster's dictionary defines a rule as "a fixed principle that determines conduct" (McKechnie, 1983, p. 1585). Let's deconstruct this definition: a rule is "fixed" meaning that it does not change regardless of the situation. In reality, we know that rules have to undergo occasional modifications in the everyday life of a classroom. Nonetheless, rules establish the boundaries for behavior (Nakamura, 2000), and consistency in their implementation is essential to effective classroom management.

Effective teachers have a minimum number of classroom rules, which tend to focus on expectations of how to act toward one another, maintain a safe environment, and participate in learning (Marzano et al., 2003; McLeod et al., 2003; Thompson, 2002). These teachers offer clear explanations of the rules, model the rules, rehearse the expectations with students, and offer students opportunities to be successful in meeting the expectations (Covino &

Iwanicki, 1996; Emmer et al., 1980). There is no magic number of rules that govern a classroom; rather, it is the clear establishment of fair, reasonable, enforceable, and consistently applied rules that makes a difference in classrooms.

Effective educators have a sense of classroom tempo and student harmony such that they are aware of when an intervention may be needed to prevent a problem (Johnson, 1997). Often, teachers use nonverbal cues, proximity, and redirection to prevent misbehavior. These techniques typically allow the momentum of the instruction to continue and refocus the student; however, there are times when a stronger intervention is necessary. When a rule is broken, an effective teacher is prepared to address the problem. Effective teachers tend to react in several ways, including the following: positive reinforcement that points to the desired behavior, consequences that punish the negative behavior, a combination of reinforcement and consequences, or indirectly responding to the behavior such that the student is reminded of why a rule is important. What an effective teacher does not do is react to an entire class for a rule infraction by a single student.

Routines

While they are more flexible than rules, routines or procedures are specific ways of doing things that, for the most part, vary little during the course of the day or the year. Classrooms typically require many routines to operate efficiently and effectively (McLeod et al., 2003). For example, routines commonly include how to enter and leave the classroom, take attendance, indicate lunch selection, secure materials, dispose of trash, label work, turn in assignments, make a transition during or between instructional activities, get to safety during drills and actual emergencies, and change from one activity or location to another. In essence, routines shape the classroom climate.

Effective teachers use routines for daily tasks more than their ineffective counterparts (Stronge, Tucker, & Ward, 2003). They invest the time at the start of the school year to teach the routines. By establishing and practicing routines that require little monitoring, teachers ensure that the focus of the classroom is more squarely on instruction (Covino & Iwanicki, 1996;

McLeod et al., 2003; Shellard & Protheroe, 2000). Effective teachers frequently provide students with cues to remind them of acceptable behavior, and effective teachers are good at organizing and maintaining a positive classroom environment (Education USA Special Report, n.d.).

The establishment of routines allows for flexibility. For example, the teacher may not rehearse with students what should occur if a new student joins the class, but might adapt the routine used for greeting classroom guests (Emmer et al., 1980). Additionally, routines empower students to be more responsible for their own behavior and learning in the classroom (Covino & Iwanicki, 1996). When classroom management issues arise, the teacher has procedures to address the concern in an efficient, fair, and consistent way (Shellard & Protheroe, 2000; Thomas & Montgomery, 1998). Thus, the result of established procedures is more time for teaching and learning.

Classroom Organization

Classroom management and organization are intertwined. While rules and routines influence student behavior, classroom organization affects the physical elements of the classroom, making it a more productive environment for its users. How the classroom environment is organized influences the behavior in it. For example, actions as simple as color-coding folders, establishing fixed locations for lab supplies, maintaining folders for students to pick up missed work after being absent, keeping extra copies of "Back to School Night" items to share with new students, and designating specific places for other classroom supplies can have a dramatic effect on classroom organization and, consequently, on student learning. While these procedures and a multitude like them are simple matters, they nonetheless can be essential components for a smoothly operating classroom.

Classroom organization is evident in a room even if no one is present. Furniture arrangements, location of materials, displays, and fixed elements are all part of organization. Effective teachers decorate the room with student work, they arrange the furniture to promote interaction as appropriate, and they have comfortable areas for working (Kohn, 1996). They also consider student needs in arranging the room by leaving space for wheelchairs to maneuver; having walkways so students can access materials, pencil sharpeners, and the trashcan with minimal disturbance to others; and organizing in such a way as to allow the teacher to freely move around the room to monitor student progress (McLeod et al., 2003).

Teachers are observers of behavior and understand the rhythm of the classroom. Placing materials near the pencil sharpener may seem like a good idea, until one considers that at the start of a lesson this area may become congested with some students retrieving materials for their group and others waiting to use the pencil sharpener. However, the pencil sharpener and the trashcan may be a good pairing if the pencil sharpener tends to break regularly, spilling its contents on the floor; this way shavings fall into the trash instead. Effective teachers think about the little details that enhance the use of available space in the classroom as well as the big issues.

Expectations for Student Behavior

Attending to issues of classroom management and organization provides the foundation for having high expectations for student behavior. Effective teachers have higher expectations for how students are to conduct themselves in the classroom than their less effective colleagues (Stronge et al., 2003). They are better managers of student behavior (Emmer et al., 1980). They establish relationships with their students in which high levels of cooperation and dominance (i.e., giving students a sense of purpose and guidance) are balanced, resulting in an optimal relationship (Marzano et al., 2003). Effective teachers teach expectations to students and reinforce the desired behaviors with their verbal and nonverbal cues. Another characteristic of effective teachers is that they hold students individually accountable (Kohn, 1996) and, if necessary, use intervention strategies to help students learn the desired behavior (McLeod et al., 2003). An exploratory study of effective and ineffective third-grade teachers found that ineffective teachers had five times as many disruptive events in an hour when compared with their more effective counterparts (Stronge et al., 2003). Through fair and consistent discipline, teachers reinforce their expectations of students and create a classroom that is focused on instruction.

Visualizing the Quality

The following graphic organizer (Figure 3.2) is one way of conceptualizing how the components of the Quality of Classroom Management and Organization fit together. "Classroom organization" captures the structural aspects of how a teacher structures his or her classroom, and "expectations for student behavior" refers to the interpersonal and conduct norms that a teacher establishes. Together these structural and interpersonal elements contribute to the overall classroom management and ultimately to the unique climate and culture of every classroom.

Focus on the Teacher

Mandrel has the desire and determination to succeed; he wants to be a good teacher. Others can see his potential, but it has yet to be fully realized, largely because he hasn't learned how to effectively manage his students. This is a hurdle he can overcome. This year, Mandrel was given a choice as to who would be his mentor. He selected a teacher with whom he has good rapport and who is willing to meet regularly with him. The tools presented in this section of the chapter can be used to identify areas of strength and weakness to support growth in the effective implementation of classroom management and organization.

FIGURE 3.2

Visual Representation of Classroom Management and Organization (Example of Fishbone Mapping)

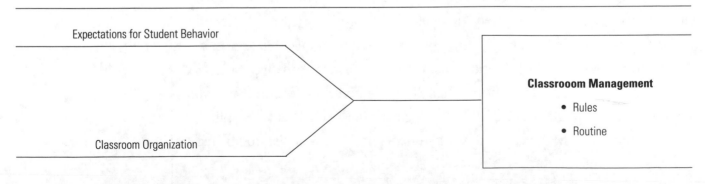

Classroom Management: Rules

Last year, Mandrel had his classroom rules, along with the consequences for not following the rules, posted for students. However, he found it difficult to get students to follow his rules. Worse yet, he knows that he did not do a very good job enforcing them. Before the new school year started, Mandrel met with his mentor to examine the classroom rules he had created. The mentor suggested organizing the rules into a table (figure 3.3) to make sure they met the criteria for being a good rule. There are four criteria that a rule needs to meet to stay on the list. The rule must be all of the following:

1. *clearly stated* so students know what is expected of them.
2. *reasonable* so students can realistically follow it.
3. *enforceable* such that Mandrel will take the time and effort to address any violations. If he is not willing to invest the effort, then the item may be too trivial or there may be a better solution.
4. *general* so that the rule addresses several behaviors as opposed to one specific misdeed.

A good rule of thumb is that the rule should be written as a positive statement so that students know what is the desired behavior. However, if something is an absolute, such as "No gum chewing," then it is simpler to just say so.

Only two of the rules in figure 3.3 meet all four criteria. The rules Mandrel created were all clearly stated in terms of the behavior. However, two of them were not reasonable because students would not be expected to follow them at all times. Of course there is some flexibility, but keeping a list of rules to a minimum will help Mandrel enforce them. When rules such as "talk in an indoor voice" are made, it is more difficult to enforce them. An "indoor voice" in one home may be at a whisper-level and in another home, it may be at a higher volume. Only two of the rules were general enough in nature so that they could be applied across multiple behaviors. It is simply not possible to regulate all behavior with written rules, so having broader ones helps to cover more behavior.

FIGURE 3.3

Classroom Rules Proposed by Mandrel

➤

Reflect on the Teacher: Case 3A

Mandrel has several rules that he feels are important; suggest ways he can consolidate or reword them.

	Proposed Rule	Clearly stated	Reason-able	Enforce-able	General	Stated Positively
1.	Respect each other.	X	X	X	X	X
2.	Be prepared to participate in class.	X	X	X	X	X
3.	Care for classroom materials and equipment as if they were yours.		X			X
4.	Talk in an indoor voice.		X			X
5.	Raise your hand for permission to talk.	X		X		X
6.	Stay in your seat at all times.	X		X		X
7.	Complete all your work on time.	X	X			X
8.	If you make a mess, clean it up.	X	X			X
9.	No eating, chewing, or drinking in class.	X	X	X		
10.	No hitting, running, or horseplay.	X	X	X		

Classroom Management: Routines

Mandrel's mentor observed him during a recent lesson. She asked Mandrel to explain the routines he used with his students in terms of taking attendance, getting materials, and turning in work. Mandrel could clearly explain his attendance/lunch request procedure and indicated that he had modeled it after the one his cooperating teacher had used during student teaching. In terms of the other two items, Mandrel said he just did what seemed to fit at the time. His mentor suggested that he build on the success he had with the lunch routine (described in the *Resources* section) by developing routines for common events in the classroom. The first step was for Mandrel to generate a list of what these recurring activities were. He then shared the list with his mentor.

Mandrel and his mentor reviewed the list. She asked him to recall what he had shared with her about the attendance/lunch routine. She asked him if

Common Classroom Occurrences

▲ Attendance

▲ Lunch counts

▲ Collecting work

▲ Returning work

▲ Distributing supplies

▲ Returning supplies

▲ Walking to specials (PE, art, music, library, computers)

▲ Morning work

▲ Make up work

▲ Afternoon dismissal

▲ Settling students down

▲ Changing activities

▲ What to do when you finish your work

▲ Drills: Fire, Tornado, Lock-down

he were absent, how the substitute teacher would know about it. Mandrel showed her his standard substitute plan information sheet that had the procedure written out. His mentor said that he could cross the first two bullets off the list since he had a routine for each of them. She asked him if there were any other items on the list that the students consistently did well. He indicated that drills, starting morning work, and walking in the hall were fine, so he crossed those off the list, too. Looking together at the list, they decided to prioritize what routines should be developed and taught early on and which ones could be added later. They focused on materials management (a combination of getting and returning materials) and changing activities as these transitional times were when Mandrel felt like he was losing time. Together they brainstormed detailed steps for each routine on an index card that Mandrel could easily reference (Figure 3.4). They talked about how he could introduce the routine and practice it with students. They agreed to meet after he introduced the first routine—changing activities. The second routine would be introduced a couple of days later. As students mastered a routine and became comfortable with it, a new one would be added.

Classroom Layout

Mandrel is a fairly well-organized teacher. Walking into his classroom, his mentor noticed that Mandrel's desk was free of clutter, his classroom displays

FIGURE 3.4
Mandrel's Changing Activities Routine Cue Card

Changing Activities
1. Get the students' attention.
Strategies: "if you can hear my voice clap once, if you can hear my voice snap twice, if you can
hear my voice…" should work in two to three actions.
Flicker the lights, play a tone on the xylophone.
Students need to know that they need to stop what they are doing and look at me for further instruction.
2. Tell the students that we are changing activities and what they need to do in a specific amount of time.
3. Let students ask questions if they have them . . . see if another student can answer it.
4. Give students the signal to change activities and time them.
5. Report back to students how well they did changing activities.

were attractive and up to date, and there were areas designated for materials and specific activities. He typically had materials prepared and lessons staged so he could go from one activity to the next. Mandrel used bins and color-coded accordion folders. He had one bin for his morning activities and another one for the afternoon. The folders held the book, papers, sample, etc. for the different subjects. His mentor noted the presence of the bins on his desk (see the *Resources* section for other organizational tips).

One area in which Mandrel needed feedback was in making the best use of his classroom layout. He has a combination of fixed features (gray items on Figure 3.5) and movable furniture. He has two main concerns: 1) students seem to gather in the back of the room near the sink and water fountain when they finish their work; and 2) he has tables that seat six students each with an open cubbie space affixed under each place on the table, so some students always have to turn their chairs around when he does whole group instruction. He currently has 21 students. Mandrel wants to be able to see his students at all times even if he is working with a group at a table or at his desk.

FIGURE 3.5
Mandrel's Current Classroom Layout

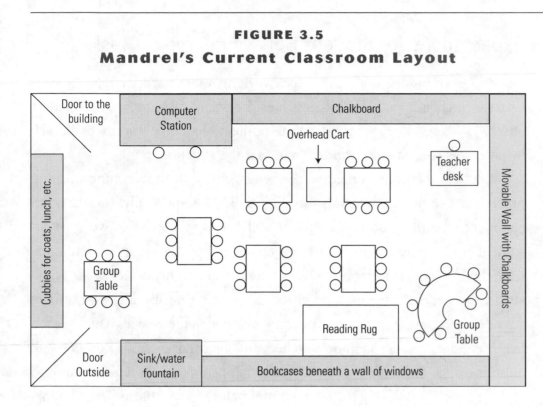

◄

Reflect on the Teacher: Case 3B

- *What can Mandrel do to eliminate some of the traffic flow problems?*

- *Suggest an alternative room arrangement that would address his concerns about students focusing on each other instead of on him when he is trying to teach. NOTE: One wildcard in this room arrangement is the movable wall. If the wall is rarely moved, then it can be used like a fixed wall; if the wall is moved more than weekly, one would want easy-to-move items along that wall. Make your own determination of how you want to deal with the wall. Use Figure 3.6 to sketch out your idea.*

FIGURE 3.6
Suggestions for Improved Room Layout

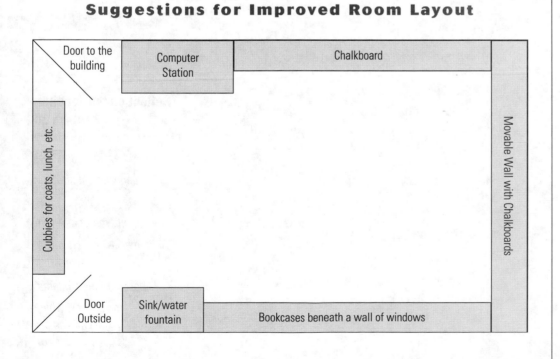

Expectations for Student Behavior: Time on Task

Mandrel and his mentor have been working on classroom management issues, which influence his expectations for student behavior. His mentor observed Mandrel's class using a time-on-task chart that captured off-task behaviors as well as how Mandrel managed the situation.

Mandrel's mentor recorded student engagement in the teaching-learning process at five-minute intervals (see Figure 3.7). Additionally, she recorded comments regarding off-task behavior and teacher responses. Two types of student behavior were recorded as off-task: 1) instances when students disrupted others and 2) instances when students were visibly disengaged. Those visibly disengaged students certainly could be thinking about class, but they are not participating in class in the same manner as their peers. During each five-minute cycle, the mentor watched and listened carefully for one full minute to get a clear sense of what was happening in the classroom, and recorded her notes during the four minutes before the next sampling of information. If Mandrel was uninvolved with students, the activity he was doing (e.g., grading papers) was noted under the "Task" column as well as what the students were doing. If the teacher takes no action to address disruptive or disengaged students, his mentor checked the box for "None."

➤

**Reflect on the Teacher:
Case 3C**

- *Describe Mandrel's management strategy.*

- *What type of interventions does he use most?*

- *Based on the students' responses, where can he improve?*

FIGURE 3.7
Time on Task Chart

Observer Janice Jones **Date** 10/17 **Teacher** Mandrel Epps **Subject** Social Studies **Number of Students** 21 **Start time** 10:45 a.m.

Interval	Task, activity, event, question	Off-Task Behaviors (Note # of students and describe behavior.)		Management Strategy		Nature of Intervention	
5 min	Transition from Reading to Social Studies (Native Americans) Gave a student a tally mark (she had been warned previously)	Disrupting Others 2	Visibly Disengaged 0	Verbal X, Nonverbal X, None o	*Comments* One student got the "eye"	Positive o, Negative X, Neutral o	*Comments* Gave Student 1 a tally mark—her name was already on the board
10 min	Sent a student with a note to the media center to get a better VCR, the one in the room had a tracking problem. Had the students tell about previous learning . . . . Iroquois mask, story sticks, maple syrup	Disrupting Others 2	Visibly Disengaged 4	Verbal X, Nonverbal X, None o	*Comments* Used proximity towards some of the disengaged students and called on others	Positive o, Negative X, Neutral o	*Comments* Took 5 minutes of Student 2's recess (already had a tally mark)
15 min	Had the students get their folders on Native Americans out and head a paper to record observations—gave directions	Disrupting Others 0	Visibly Disengaged 1	Verbal o, Nonverbal o, None X	*Comments*	Positive o, Negative o, Neutral o	*Comments*
20 min	The video was playing	Disrupting Others 1	Visibly Disengaged 0	Verbal X, Nonverbal o, None o	*Comments* Student 3 made fun of an actor's appearance, saying "Look at Grandma"	Positive X, Negative o, Neutral o	*Comments* Reminded students that this was a legend, so people may look different
25 min	The video was playing	Disrupting Others 0	Visibly Disengaged 2	Verbal o, Nonverbal o, None X	*Comments* Students 4 & 5 were off task, but the teacher's back was towards them	Positive o, Negative o, Neutral o	*Comments* The teacher took no action
30 min	The video was playing	Disrupting Others 0	Visibly Disengaged 4	Verbal o, Nonverbal X, None o	*Comments* Lots of laughter in one section	Positive o, Negative o, Neutral X	*Comments* Students refocused

FIGURE 3.7
Time on Task Chart (continued)

Interval	Task, activity, event, question	Off-Task Behaviors (Note # of students and describe behavior.)		Management Strategy		Nature of Intervention	
35 min	"Let's share some observations of Native Americans, first from the past and then we will do the present based on what you saw in the video"	Disrupting Others 1 Visibly Disengaged 7		Verbal X Nonverbal 0 None 0	*Comments* Said "I need everyone's attention, if you hear my voice clap once" (Routine we worked on earlier)	Positive X Negative 0 Neutral 0	*Comments* Thanked students for focusing so quickly
40 min	Talked about how some students were surprised that Native Americans are still alive today . . . cleared up some misunderstandings	Disrupting Others 0 Visibly Disengaged 0		Verbal 0 Nonverbal 0 None 0	*Comments*	Positive 0 Negative 0 Neutral 0	*Comments*
45 min	Continued discussion about Native Americans today	Disrupting Others 0 Visibly Disengaged 2		Verbal 0 Nonverbal X None 0	*Comments* Student 2 and Student 6 were playing with their sweaters	Positive 0 Negative 0 Neutral X	*Comments* The students stopped
50 min	Praised students for doing a good job . . . some students clapped and cheered, but gained on-task behavior quickly	Disrupting Others 0 Visibly Disengaged 0		Verbal X Nonverbal 0 None 0	*Comments*	Positive X Negative 0 Neutral 0	*Comments*
55 min	Moved right into mathematics lesson on subtraction with regrouping . . . very smooth transition	Disrupting Others 0 Visibly Disengaged 0		Verbal 0 Nonverbal 0 None 0	*Comments*	Positive 0 Negative 0 Neutral 0	*Comments*

Notes:
Disrupting others would include students who are not only off task but also attempting to distract others from the teacher-assigned tasks.
Visibly disengaged would include students who are daydreaming, doodling, staring out the window or otherwise not focusing on the teacher's assigned tasks, but who are not distracting other students.
Management strategy would be any action taken by the teacher either in response to a lack of attention by students or in anticipation of possible disruptions.
Nature of intervention would include positive responses such as praising students who are attending or participating, negative responses such as yelling at students, or neutral responses such as changing the activity or moving near the student or students.
Under *Comments*, note the type of action taken or what was said.

Making Connections

Consider the Scenario

Reread the teacher scenario at the beginning of this chapter and the bits of information shared on the form with examples about Mandrel, the fictitious teacher in the scenario. Consider the questions below.

Using the space below, summarize what positive teacher behaviors and actions exist, and what performance areas need improvement for Mandrel.

Positive Attributes	Areas for Improvement

What descriptor best describes Mandrel's skills in the area of "classroom management and organization"?

_____ Master: demonstrates the complexity of the quality resulting in a rich learning experience for students

_____ Professional: demonstrates the quality most of the time so there is a productive learning experience for students

_____ Apprentice: demonstrates the quality well-enough for learning to occur, but performance is inconsistent

_____ Undeveloped: demonstrates sub-par performance of the quality

Why did you select a particular descriptor?

How could Mandrel's performance be improved?

Reflecting on My Current Performance

Rate your own performance on the qualities associated with classroom management and organization using the explanation of each major quality highlighted in the chapter.

	Undeveloped	Apprentice	Professional	Master
Classroom Management				
Classroom Organization				
Expectations for Student Behavior				

Reflection Learning Log

What do I better understand now after studying and reflecting on classroom management and organization?

What are next steps to improve my performance?

What resources (e.g., people and materials) are needed to enhance my teaching effectiveness?

Resources

This section contains three items:

▲ further elaboration on issues raised in the discussion of Mandrel's case,

▲ the *Authors' Perspective,* and

▲ *blackline masters* of forms that can be used to promote improvement and reflection on qualities of effective teachers.

Follow-up Explanation of Mandrel's Attendance/ Lunch Routine

On the first day of school, students were given a piece of paper the size of a business card that was affixed to a magnet of the same size (available at most office supply stores). They were told to write their first name and last initial in big letters on the card. Then students decorated the cards with a picture of their favorite activity to do outside of school. Mandrel had students introduce themselves by talking about their card. Then he had them find at least one other person in the class with whom they shared an interest. Finally, he explained the attendance/lunch procedure. When students arrive each day, their magnets are all on the magnetic chalkboard in the "Welcome" column. Before students even put away their bags and coats, they move their magnet to the appropriate lunch choice column (Figure 3.8). Then, after morning

FIGURE 3.8
Mandrel's Attendance/Lunch Chart*

Welcome	Buying Lunch	Buying Milk	Brought Lunch

*It is made using colored tape to form the outline, and the labels are on magnets. This makes it easy to remove in order to clean the chalkboard.

announcements, Mandrel takes attendance by seeing whose magnet has not been moved and counts the number of students who are buying lunch.

Mandrel also shared that he lines up students for lunch by calling for the students who are buying lunch or milk to be in the front of the line, so they can continue ahead in the cafeteria to the food service line while he leads the rest of the students to their assigned table. He had not thought of this as a routine, just something he did that worked. His mentor commented that this worked well and he could build from this experience to enhance the operation of other parts of the instructional day. Additional organizational tips that work across grade levels are included in Figure 3.9.

Reflect on the Teacher: Authors' Perspective

The *Reflect on the Teacher* questions are provided to encourage interactive and reflective reading and application of the *Handbook for Qualities of Effective Teachers*. In most cases there are no right or wrong answers. The *Authors' Perspective* is provided as one way to reflect on the information presented.

Reflect on the Teacher: Case 3A (see p. 72)

Mandrel has several rules that he feels are important. Suggest ways he can consolidate or reword them.

Group rules (Figure 3.3, p. 72) according to their commonalities.

▲ Rules 3, 8, and 9 address the classroom environment. He could combine the rules to create a new rule: "Keep the classroom and materials neat." In the explanation of the rule, Mandrel can explain that this includes no eating because crumbs and sticky substances tend to get everywhere even when someone is being careful.

▲ Rule 1 ("Respect each other") is broad enough to incorporate the safety issues in Rule 10 as well as the need to keep voice volume at an appropriate level so everyone can learn (Rule 4). Rules 5 and 6 are about respecting the teacher's authority in the classroom. This could

FIGURE 3.9

Organizational Tips

Materials	If students commonly work in the same group, assign each group a container (dish tubs, baskets, and trays work well) that they can send one member to retrieve and return for each activity. It gives the students an incentive to treat the common supplies well.
	Place scissors, tape, stapler, hole punch, calculators, rulers, and other commonly needed items in a common place that students can access on their own.
	Have a can of sharpened pencils near the pencil sharpener. If the lead breaks during class, a student can place the pencil in the can and retrieve a sharpened one. At a more appropriate time (e.g., end of the lesson) the student can return the borrowed pencil and sharpen the one that was left (Thompson, 2002). HINT: The teacher may not have to buy the initial pencils, since pencils frequently can be found on the floor when they have rolled away under another desk. Just tell your custodian where retrieved pencils can be placed for student use.
	Keep extra school supplies on hand for students who forget or run out of their own. Also, this is helpful when a new student arrives in class who may not have all the supplies needed.
	Set up numbered work stations with necessary supplies and assign students to matching work groups. This works well when students must go to the equipment (e.g., science lab) versus taking the equipment to their desks.
Work Assignments	Set up collection trays for finished work labeled with either the subject for elementary classrooms or periods for secondary classrooms.
	Create wall organizers with identified bins for class assignments so that students can pick up missed work after a late arrival or an absence.
Lesson Plans	At the secondary level when there are multiple preps separated by brief breaks, it can be helpful to have a plastic file folder holder affixed to the wall so the teacher can pull the necessary folder.
	Keep plans in a binder that has divider pages for the different subjects/periods. Use plastic page protectors to hold copies of handouts and transparencies (make sure to have the "crystal clear" sleeves or else the transparency will have to be removed from the sleeve).
	Organize lesson plans electronically. If the room is equipped with a monitor for PowerPoint presentations, use the first slide to identify the title and the second slide the goals; this not only organizes the students, but also reminds the teacher as well.

Figure continues

FIGURE 3.9

Organizational Tips (continued)

Emergency Procedures	Post fire and tornado information in the room. Include labeled maps of where to go when exiting the classroom for tornado and fire drills/emergencies.
	Know the location of the nearest fire extinguisher and fire alarm pull.
	Train students to know what to do in an emergency situation.
	Clearly label the office call button so substitute teachers can immediately identify it if an emergency occurs.
	Keep a list of all students who may require medical attention in your grade book. Know the protocol for what to do, for example, diabetics, bee stings, epileptic seizures, etc. As appropriate, alert substitute teachers.
	If in a specific-use classroom, such as science, know how to operate the eyewash station and shower, the location of the emergency shut-off valves in the room, and where safety equipment is stored.
Schedules	Display a poster with the basic flow of the day (i.e., bell changes in secondary school or in elementary school when reading, math, resource classes, lunch, science, social studies, etc. occur).
	Write a daily agenda for students to know what to expect in terms of the day's objective (see *Chapter 5* on writing informational objectives), activities, and homework. Note any changes in the regular daily schedule in this location.
	Create a Web page with weekly assignments listed and hyperlinks to possible resources.
Classroom Displays	Have a board for "works in progress" where students can post work on which they want constructive criticism from their peers (Thompson, 2002). Students wind up keeping this board ever changing.
	Use a blend of student-made and commercial products to display on the walls. An art portfolio works well to keep posters flat and poster board can be tabbed with headings of different units, so the teacher can pull out new material as appropriate for display.

be addressed under Rule 1: Students should respect the teacher as well as their classmates.

▲ Rule 7 can be included in the explanation of what it means to be prepared for class.

The overall suggestion would be to keep Rules 1 and 2 and add one new rule about classroom neatness.

Reflect on the Teacher: Case 3B (see p. 75)

What can Mandrel do to eliminate some of the traffic flow problems?

The classroom has a lot of "attractive nuisances" in the back of the room near the sink area. There are two group worktables, a reading space, bookcases, and the cubbies all in the back half of the room. Part of Mandrel's challenge is the physical space arrangement; the other part of the challenge is classroom management. If traffic is a problem, limit the number of students who may be at any of those locations after they finish their work. There seems to be more potential for congestion on the left-hand side of the room and in the back than in the front or to the right. Additionally, the group worktable near the cubbies is in the way when students line up to exit from either door. One way to avoid this problem is to move the work table to another location so that students can line up a few feet out from the cubbies.

Suggest an alternative room arrangement that would address his concerns about students focusing on each other instead of on him when he is trying to teach.

Mandrel has three of the five tables oriented so no students have to turn around to look at him. So in rearranging the room, the other two could be flipped. This will create less space from the front wall to the back wall so the other furniture will have to be moved around. There are various pros and cons to placing the teacher's desk in the front of the room. By placing the desk in the back of the room, Mandrel is still able to see his students, but he has now created a space where he can work individually with a student without having the student or himself in the class' spotlight. These are the two main changes we suggest. As for the other suggestions, a lot depends on personal preference for how spaces work.

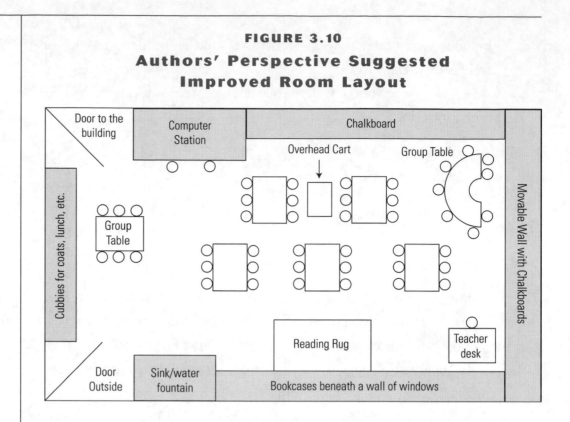

FIGURE 3.10

Authors' Perspective Suggested Improved Room Layout

Reflect on the Teacher: Case 3C (see p. 76)

Describe Mandrel's management strategy.

Mandrel does not seem to have a clear preference between verbal or nonverbal responses. However, he tends to use verbal interventions when students are being disruptive or have the potential to disrupt the learning of others. The nonverbal approaches are used to refocus students.

What type of interventions does he use most?

While Mandrel uses positive, negative, and neutral interventions about equally, he tends to focus on the positive a bit more. In the cases where he used negative interventions, the students had already been warned about their behavior—it was noted on the chart that the students already had their names on the board.

Based on the students' responses, where can he improve?

At 50 minutes, Mandrel praised the students for their work. They responded with cheering that was short, and they quickly refocused. The students made a smooth transition to the next activity. When the class was recognized for behaving appropriately, it seemed to encourage more of the desired behavior. Perhaps Mandrel could try praising desired behaviors instead of relying so heavily on tally marks.

Blackline Masters

The following blackline masters can be photocopied and used in your school or district.

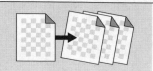

Classroom Rules Criteria

	Proposed Rule	Clearly stated	Reason-able	Enforce-able	General	Stated Positively

Classroom Arrangement

1) Take an inventory of the movable furniture/items in the room. There is space provided for additional items.

_____ Student Desks w/chairs

_____ Teacher's Desk w/chair

_____ Overhead Projector

_____ Computer(s)

_____ File Cabinet

_____ Work table(s)

_____ Bookcase(s)

_____ _____

_____ _____

_____ _____

2) Make a sketch of the classroom's fixed elements in the space provided. If the room is not rectangular, shade off areas to reflect the classroom space. In your sketch, include
   - Door(s)
   - Window(s)

- Chalkboards/whiteboards
- Mounted TV monitors
- Computer stations
- Bookcases
- Storage cabinets
- Lab stations
- Sinks
- Pencil sharpener

3) Determine how the room will be primarily used (e.g., lecture, discussion, group work).

4) Use dotted lines to show key walkways or spaces that need to stay open.

5) The biggest grouping of furniture is the student desks and chairs. Place them on the layout first. They can be moved about later on the diagram as needed, but they do encompass the largest area in most classrooms.

6) Sketch in the other furniture items.

Time on Task Chart

Observer _____ Date _____ Teacher _____ Subject _____ Number of Students _____ Start time _____

Interval	Task, activity, event, question	Off-Task Behaviors (Note # of students and describe behavior.)	Management Strategy		Nature of Intervention	
5 min		Disrupting Others _____ Visibly Disengaged _____	Verbal o Nonverbal o None o	Comments	Positive o Negative o Neutral o	Comments
10 min		Disrupting Others _____ Visibly Disengaged _____	Verbal o Nonverbal o None o	Comments	Positive o Negative o Neutral o	Comments
15 min		Disrupting Others _____ Visibly Disengaged _____	Verbal o Nonverbal o None o	Comments	Positive o Negative o Neutral o	Comments
20 min		Disrupting Others _____ Visibly Disengaged _____	Verbal o Nonverbal o None o	Comments	Positive o Negative o Neutral o	Comments
25 min		Disrupting Others _____ Visibly Disengaged _____	Verbal o Nonverbal o None o	Comments	Positive o Negative o Neutral o	Comments
30 min		Disrupting Others _____ Visibly Disengaged _____	Verbal o Nonverbal o None o	Comments	Positive o Negative o Neutral o	Comments

Time on Task Chart (continued)

Interval	Task, activity, event, question	Off-Task Behaviors (Note # of students and describe behavior.)	Management Strategy		Nature of Intervention	
35 min		Disrupting Others _____ Visibly Disengaged _____	Verbal ○ Nonverbal ○ None ○	Comments	Positive ○ Negative ○ Neutral ○	Comments
40 min		Disrupting Others _____ Visibly Disengaged _____	Verbal ○ Nonverbal ○ None ○	Comments	Positive ○ Negative ○ Neutral ○	Comments
45 min		Disrupting Others _____ Visibly Disengaged _____	Verbal ○ Nonverbal ○ None ○	Comments	Positive ○ Negative ○ Neutral ○	Comments
50 min		Disrupting Others _____ Visibly Disengaged _____	Verbal ○ Nonverbal ○ None ○	Comments	Positive ○ Negative ○ Neutral ○	Comments
55 min		Disrupting Others _____ Visibly Disengaged _____	Verbal ○ Nonverbal ○ None ○	Comments	Positive ○ Negative ○ Neutral ○	Comments

Notes:

Disrupting others would include students who are not only off task but also attempting to distract others from the teacher-assigned tasks.

Visibly disengaged would include students who are daydreaming, doodling, staring out the window or otherwise not focusing on the teacher's assigned tasks, but who are not distracting other students.

Management strategy would be any action taken by the teacher either in response to a lack of attention by students or in anticipation of possible disruptions.

Nature of intervention would include positive responses such as praising students who are attending or participating, negative responses such as yelling at students, or neutral responses such as changing the activity or moving near the student or students.

Under *Comments*, note the type of action taken or what was said.

ORGANIZING FOR INSTRUCTION

Jin-Ah Ko has taught biology for 17 years. Last year, her school was mandated by the school district to adopt an alternate-day block schedule, which previously had been adopted by all the other high schools in the district. The teachers who liked having daily 47-minute periods with their students had opposed this move. So now, Jin-Ah sees her students every other day for 90 minutes. Historically, her students have done very well on the annual state assessment, but last year her scores were lower. While students are different every year, the other two biology teachers' class scores did not change as much as Jin-Ah's scores. The main difference among the teachers seems to be how the teachers have adjusted their lessons to match the new time configuration. Jin-Ah's main adjustment for the new block schedule was to squeeze two of her traditional lessons together into one block period.

Research Summary

Interestingly, the work of teachers and the work of research scientists have a number of similarities. Both teachers and research scientists have public components to their work, such as the daily classroom instruction or the announcement of a ground-breaking discovery. Both do a significant amount of preparation behind the scenes. Teachers make long-range and daily plans to optimize the time they have with students, while scientists develop research plans and spend months and even years hypothesizing, testing, securing funding, and analyzing. For both groups, at any moment, there can be a last-minute change that affects the well-constructed plan. We obviously know that the work of scientists is technical and complex; it's time we recognized that high-quality teaching is an art and a science, too. Being a successful teacher is a complex undertaking and not for the haphazardly prepared.

This chapter highlights how effective teachers organize for instruction by creating the maximum learning time and opportunities for students. Specifically, effective teacher research on the quality of organizing for instruction focuses on these factors:

▲ *Focusing on Instruction.* Instruction is the primary purpose for school. Effective teachers know the very reason for schooling is teaching and learning. And, in their classrooms, these educators maintain an intense focus on instruction (Peart & Campbell, 1999; Shellard & Protheroe, 2000; Walker, 1998).

▲ *Maximizing Instructional Time.* Classrooms are busy places where teachers are given a finite amount of time for teaching their subject(s). Effective teachers are able to qualitatively do more with the same amount of time than their less effective counterparts (Cruickshank & Haefele, 2001).

▲ *Expecting Students to Achieve.* The self-fulfilling prophecy can hold true when working with students. If teachers convey the message that they expect students to do their best and grow academically, students will respond positively because they are in a supportive environment (Covino & Iwanicki, 1996).

▲ *Planning and Preparing for Instruction.* Effective teachers invest the time and effort needed to develop instructional plans and materials that meet individual students' needs (Shellard & Protheroe, 2000).

Figure 4.1 provides a visual overview of the chapter. Following an elaboration of the four key quality indicators associated with organizing for instruction, tools to enhance effectiveness are presented in the context of our fictional teacher, Jin-Ah. The questions posed in the *Focus on the Teacher* section are addressed at the end of the chapter, followed by the presentation of blackline masters.

FIGURE 4.1

Chapter Overview

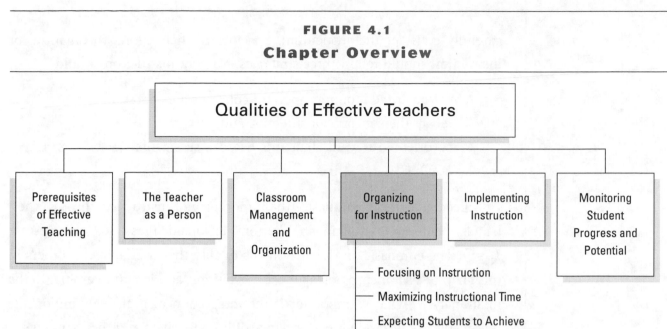

Focusing on Instruction

Effective teachers approach instruction with a focus that rivals an athlete getting ready for competition. Athletes do not just show up and compete; rather, they prepare consistently over time, refining their plan as the event nears. And, if they believe in their goal and that their plan will succeed, they translate their plan into actions. In the classroom, teachers organize for instruction in much the same way, although their plans focus on academics (Covino & Iwanicki, 1996).

Organization does not just occur; teachers use multiple levels of planning, such as yearly, term, unit, weekly, and daily plans, to ensure that knowledge, concepts, and skills are presented in a sequential manner with adequate time for both teaching and learning (Burden & Byrd, 1994; Thompson, 2002). When planning for instruction, teachers create an overview of each unit, identifying components that are primary, secondary, enrichment, and remediation (Thompson, 2002). In this way teachers have preselected what must be taught and what can be used to supplement instruction. In deciding what will be the essential instructional focus in their classes, teachers need to carefully consider the curriculum. Specifically, their efforts to organize for instruction should reflect three strategies. Namely, instruction should

▲ be organized around important concepts and questions,

▲ reflect the concerns of students, and

▲ be oriented toward standards-based assessments (Jackson & Davis, 2000, p. 43).

Effective teachers emphasize the importance of instruction through their beliefs, planning, and actions (Wharton-McDonald, Pressley, & Hampston, 1998). The emphasis on instruction is a quality that overlaps with others in this chapter, as it incorporates time, expectations, and lesson planning. In the final analysis, what is important is the integration of multiple components that result in outstanding performance of both teachers and their students.

Maximizing Instructional Time

Time is a nonrenewable resource in the classroom. Teachers only have a finite amount of it, and when it is gone there is no way to generate more. Many classrooms have schedules posted in them with bells or activity changes noted, but the actual time use during the instructional block often is not specified. A very noticeable difference between effective teachers and their less effective counterparts is that effective teachers do more with their time (Cruickshank & Haefele, 2001). There is a rhythm to the classroom resulting in quantitative and qualitative differences in the learning. One strategy that effective teachers use is the investment of time at the beginning of the year to establish routines and expectations that help them conserve their time so that minutes are not lost on transitions or disruptions.

An important step in establishing expectations is the development of relationships with students. Over two decades ago, Emmer, Evertson, and Anderson (1980) observed that more effective teachers spent a greater amount of time getting to know their students on the first day of school. These teachers sent a message to students that they were important—and the effectiveness of this strategy has been reinforced in the subsequent research literature (e.g., Collinson, Killeavy, & Stephenson, 1999; Peart & Campbell,

1999) as well as by our own common sense. Building a solid foundation of relationships in the classroom helps to create a collaborative and supportive environment that operates more smoothly.

Furthermore, effective teachers are adept at conserving time. For example, they have routines to facilitate transitions and carefully targeted questioning strategies to make better use of the limited time they have with students (Covino & Iwanicki, 1996). (Questioning strategies will be discussed in greater detail in Chapter 5.) Classroom routines clearly help teachers maximize learning time and may be classified in four ways, according to Burden and Byrd (1994):

▲ *Activity* routines are used to engage students in practicing specific skills. The location and time of these activities are standardized and modeled until the activity occurs without much direction from the teacher on the mechanics of it. Repetition transforms many typical classroom activities from novel to routine events. Activity-related routines facilitate the movement of students and smooth transitions. Instead of telling students to report to various groups, the teacher may just announce that it is time for writer's workshop and students know where in the classroom to go to start on their work. Other examples include reading groups, science labs, and physical education warm-up exercises.

▲ *Instructional* routines relate to the procedures used with particular instructional strategies and methods. For example, students may be taught the specific steps involved in the strategy of "Think, Pair, Share" (an instructional strategy where a student *thinks*, then *pairs* with another student to exchange thoughts, and *shares* with the larger group). With each successive opportunity to "Think, Pair, Share," students will become more comfortable with the strategy. Thus, instructional routines become linked to specific strategies. The use of instructional routines shifts the emphasis from how the instruction is delivered to the content that is addressed.

▲ *Management* routines establish order in the classroom, such as how to:

- indicate if students are buying the school lunch,
- walk in the hall,
- pass out materials and collect them when done,
- let the teacher know that help is needed, and
- dismiss students from the class.

These routines reduce the administrative and transitional time spent in the classroom. They are not academic in nature.

▲ *Executive Planning* routines assist teachers when planning for instruction. It is the planning format that is followed, such as looking at the curriculum standards, reviewing last year's notes on the lesson, aligning the curriculum with planned assessments, identifying resources, making an instructional materials list, and sequencing lesson activities. This routine focuses on establishing a pattern for how one plans so that all the necessary components are addressed. It is like the scientific method in that there is an order and fixed elements so that one considers each piece.

The first three routine types relate directly to the expectations that teachers have for the time they spend with students; the fourth, "Executive Planning," focuses on teachers making better use of their limited planning time. Later in this chapter, we will discuss elements of lesson planning in more depth. Establishing routines is one way of letting students know what is expected from them in specific situations. However, the reason why effective teachers use routines goes beyond classroom management; more specifically and more importantly, effective teachers use routines to make the most of classroom time for teaching and learning.

Expecting Students to Achieve

Teacher expectations for student success are powerful motivators for both the teacher and the student. For students to achieve at the highest levels, teachers need to set appropriate goals with students and support them in attaining their goals. Effective teachers convey a "you can do it" attitude to students and demonstrate confidence in the students' abilities to master new content and skills (Covino & Iwanicki, 1996; Peart & Campbell, 1999; Walberg, 1984).

Goals

Effective teachers communicate high expectations to all students (Johnson, 1997). Setting high expectations and supporting students in achieving them is a means to close an achievement gap among students (Freel, 1998). Researchers have found that top students receive more attention and higher expectations from their teachers than students in the bottom third of their class, so teachers need to be aware of potential biases (Good & Brophy, 1997). Consequently, expectations must be realistic and reasonable for each student to accomplish during the time spent with the teacher (Brown, 2002). Teachers who assume responsibility for student learning and set high expectations for all of their students are generally more successful (Corbett, Wilson, & Williams, 2002; Jussim & Eccles, 1992).

Support

Having high expectations is not enough to ensure student success. Teachers must actively engage students and demonstrate their commitment to student achievement through their whole-hearted dedication to teaching (Mason, Schroeter, Combs, & Washington, 1992). Mastering essential concepts is expected for all students, but effective teachers use more than mastery; they issue challenges. Students will work for teachers whom they perceive as believing in their abilities. Moreover, higher achievement standards are hallmarks of the effective teacher's classroom (Education USA Special Report, n.d.). Clearly, the power of an effective teacher is in helping students master material they would have never been able to do on their own. They empower students to take responsibility for learning as part of their commitment to ensuring students' success (Covino & Iwanicki, 1996; Johnson, 1997). These effective educators establish a climate of trust where praise is authentic and criticism is constructive. "Increasingly, trust is recognized as a vital element. . . . Trust is necessary for effective cooperation and communication" (Tschannen-Moran & Hoy, 2000, p. 349). Effective teachers expect more of students and, in turn, raise students expectations for success (Entwisle &

Webster, 1973; Mason et al., 1992). And, consistent with our focus on organizing for instruction, helping students meet and exceed expectations must be linked to the instructional plan.

Planning and Preparing for Instruction

In classrooms where students consistently experience success, the teacher invariably has done complex, behind-the-scenes work to plan for instruction. Another way to think of planning is as decision making. Planning helps teachers with the following activities:

▲ focusing on the purpose for the lesson;
▲ reviewing the subject matter and available resources before presenting it to students; and
▲ determining how to start, deliver, and assess the lesson (Airasian, 1994).

Effective teachers spend a great deal of time deciding *how* they will teach, as they know that well-constructed plans typically yield better quality academic time because behavioral concerns diminish when students are engaged (Shellard & Protheroe, 2000). There is a growing trend for schools to encourage teachers to plan together by providing time for team planning or department-level planning. This collaborative approach reduces the isolation that teachers may feel, provides models for novice teachers, and creates a synergy of ideas. Nonetheless, many teachers engage in lesson planning alone at night and on the weekends. Regardless of how the planning is done, effective teachers consider the required curriculum, long-range and short-term perspectives, available materials, and student needs in their planning for instruction.

As any educator will recognize, students come to school at various states of readiness and developmental levels. Effective teachers meet students where they are and provide experiences to take them to higher levels of knowing. It is not sufficient for teachers to simply present material without considering where the students are in their development. Clearly, instructional objectives and supporting activities must be appropriate for the learner (Marzano,

Pickering, & McTighe, 1993). Effective teachers reflect on the instruction they are planning to ensure that the lesson 1) meets student needs, 2) is at a pace that enables students to learn the material, and 3) provides feedback to let teachers know whether students understood the content (Cruickshank & Haefele, 2001).

The activities in the classroom need to be sequenced in a manner that promotes students' cognitive and developmental growth (Panusuk, Stone, & Todd, 2002). Some lessons may be appropriate at the end of the school year that would not work as effectively in the beginning of the year if students lack prerequisite knowledge or skills, such as fine motor coordination or an ability to abstractly think about algebra-related skill sets. Thus, the lesson should match the intended learning outcomes and be paced such that students can achieve those outcomes. The effective teacher allows the lesson to evolve so that adjustments can be made based on circumstances, including on-the-spot classroom feedback from the students (Education USA Special Report, n.d.; Panusuk et al.). In summary, selecting the appropriate objective, lesson, and pace is a complex and vital component of teaching.

Key components of effective instructional planning include knowledge of the curriculum, proper selection of instructional materials and resources, and attention to both long-term and short-range planning. Each of these components will be discussed in turn.

Knowledge of the Curriculum

"Expert knowledge is organized around important concepts, the big ideas, not isolated facts" (Bransford, Brown, & Cocking, 1999, p. 9). Curriculum is the framework from which teachers draw to identify these important concepts and to focus on desired learning outcomes. Furthermore, "curriculum defines the specifics of *what* students should learn: the concepts and generalizations, the related topics and facts, and the skills and habits of mind that will enable learning" (Jackson & Davis, 2000, p. 40). Effective teachers have a deep knowledge of their content area (Covino & Iwanicki, 1996) and are able to balance competing demands as they provide a rich but well-grounded curriculum for students. They also plan lessons to allow students to use their knowledge in new and authentic ways (Marzano et al., 1993).

Teachers' plans need to be aligned with the state, school district, and school-adopted curriculum. Curriculum alignment ensures a link between what the state or district intends for students to learn, what teachers teach and assess, and what students actually learn (Walker, 1998). In a time of high-stakes testing, the curriculum addressed in the classroom needs to be aligned with the skills and knowledge to be tested in order to promote student achievement and learning equity (Hirsh, 2000). Even without high-stakes assessment systems, good teachers still align classroom plans with intended outcomes.

Instructional Materials and Resources

Effective teachers continually add to their repertoire of knowledge about instructional materials and equipment in order to meet the needs of their students. They use their knowledge of instructional standards to guide their decision making on what resources they need to acquire or develop (Buttram & Waters, 1997). Most teachers use supplementary materials and overheads on a regular basis. An increasing number of school districts are infusing schools and classrooms with computers and information technology. While the extant research has not expressly linked effective teachers and technology use, at least one report indicates that when computer technology was used, student learning increased (ISTE, n.d.). Teachers use technology to offer more individualized attention to students, increase hands-on instruction, and create a student-focused environment (Dickson & Irving, 2002; Holahan, Jurkat, & Friedman, 2000). Note: While technology was singled out here as an example, it represents just one of the many resources that teachers use to support students in learning.

Long-range Planning

Consider long-range planning to be like a blueprint which effective teachers use to consider the broad picture when planning and sequencing instruction. Long-range planning considers key issues such as curriculum standards and student needs. This planning process may occur by the year or the semester as teachers look at the big picture (Burden & Byrd, 1994; Thompson, 2002). Effective teachers are aware of how the content fits together. Also, they take into account common student misconceptions that affect lessons. Long-range planning enables high-performing teachers to integrate their instruction with that of other educators and develop interdisciplinary units. By knowing where the class will be going instructionally, teachers can plan units to connect in a seamless fashion (McEwan, 2002). In addition, by allocating time to planning, teachers can prioritize instructional goals and allocate time appropriately during the instructional days they have.

A more concise, specific level of long-range planning is the instructional unit plan, which attempts to capture the big picture for instruction over several weeks. Unit planning provides an opportunity for teachers to consider what specific objectives will be taught, how much time should be allocated to each objective, what ways students will further their understanding of the concepts, and how to assess the students (Thompson, 2002). Additionally, effective teachers use all available data such as pre-assessments and knowledge of students to assist in outlining how the instruction will be delivered (Gronlund, 2003; Thompson, 2002). Unit planning is the time when the teacher begins brainstorming, collects and organizes a variety of materials, and makes the initial determination of how to address the specific content. At this stage of planning, the teacher needs to consider the relationship between the instructional process and assessment. If a unit test or culminating assignment is to be administered at the end, then the teacher needs to develop it in the beginning to ensure that the intended learning outcomes, the instruction to be delivered, and the assessment are aligned (Gronlund, 2003).

Short-term Planning

Short-term planning refers to daily and weekly planning. Effective teachers use long-range plans to determine approximately where they should be in order to meet their objectives. Short-term plans are the physical manifestation of the mental preparation teachers undergo in planning for their students. It demonstrates their knowledge of the content (Chapter 1), understanding of students (Chapter 2), consideration of the classroom's organization (Chapter 3), instructional resources (Chapter 4), appropriate instructional strategies (Chapter 5), and assessments (Chapter 6). In essence, good planning calls on the whole gamut of extensive professional knowledge that effective teachers possess.

Weekly lesson plans, in contrast to unit plans, are developed closer to when the actual instruction will occur. A good recommendation for new teachers is to do this level of planning two weeks in advance (Thompson, 2002). Unfortunately, this is not always possible. Developing the plans at least one week ahead of time allows teachers to reflect on student progress during the previous week and modify lesson plans in response to it (Burden & Byrd, 1994). These short-term plans include details that may not have been available when the unit plan was developed, such as school-wide assemblies, instruction needed for a large group of students who were out with the flu, current events, and consideration of other needs.

Daily lesson plans are the elaboration of the weekly plan. They provide day-by-day information on the objectives, materials, strategies, and assessments that will be used. Universal daily lesson plan formats do not exist; however, an adequate daily lesson plan should be understandable to another teaching professional (Roe & Ross, 2002). Experienced educators and researchers (Burden & Byrd, 1994; Roe & Ross, 2002; Thompson, 2002) suggest the following common elements: teacher's name, date, topic area, period/time, objectives, specific content, materials, instructional strategies, student activities, alternative assignments, assessment, and homework. Alternative assignments refer to the "over planning" teachers do in the event that the lesson flows more quickly than expected or some students finish early. Alternative assignments are not busy work; they are meaningful extensions of the lesson. Ideally, lesson plan models should include suggestions for differentiation of instruction or accommodations to meet individual student learning needs. Daily lesson plans specifically state what will be done, what materials are needed, and how teachers will know whether students have learned the objective(s).

Teachers know that planning and preparation are essential, but planning is not a 100 percent guarantee that classroom instruction will go exactly as desired. The classroom is a dynamic, constantly changing environment. There are times when the plans need to be modified, sometimes almost instantaneously. For example, when teachable moments, unannounced fire drills, illnesses, unexpected assemblies, and a host of other unanticipated events occur, effective teachers adapt to the moment. How the teacher responds is critical to maintaining the momentum of instruction. When teachers go through the mental exercise of planning and organizing for instruction, they know what is important—and they are better able to adapt when needed.

Visualizing the Quality

The quality of organizing for instruction can be thought of as incorporating these four major areas: expecting students to achieve, focusing on instruction, maximizing instructional time, and planning and preparing for instruction. Each of these components can be further defined by the elements noted in figure 4.2 below. While this analytical dissection is useful for description and discussion purposes, it is the dynamic integration of expertise in these areas that is the hallmark of an effective teacher.

FIGURE 4.2

Spider Map of Organizing for Instruction

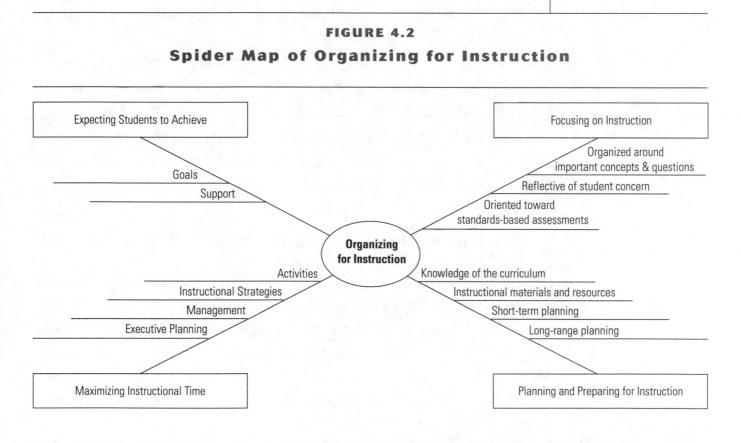

Focus on the Teacher

Jin-Ah is a respected teacher in her building and school district. She has been recognized as an outstanding science educator by the state's association of science teachers. Nonetheless, last year was a tough year for Jin-Ah; not only did the school go to a new schedule, but also she was asked to head the new biology textbook adoption committee and teach the Advanced Placement biology course (a new offering for the school). These changes were in addition to all the other personal and professional responsibilities that Jin-Ah had. She was not pleased with her students' performance and is looking for ways to improve the effectiveness of her instruction during the 90-minute block while continuing to maintain what has worked in the past.

How to Maximize Instructional Time

A student observer from a local university was assigned to visit Jin-Ah's room once a week for six weeks. After the second visit to the classroom, the student observer sat down to talk with Jin-Ah about what she saw during 4th period biology class (Figure 4.3).

If Jin-Ah had not had a university student observer, she could have asked a colleague or student teacher to record her time use, or she could have done it herself by videotaping the class and watching it later. The *Resources* section at the end of the chapter includes a brief overview of the block scheduling research and a section on how professional development supports teachers making the transition to using their time differently.

Planning and Preparing for Instruction: Alignment

Some school districts choose to develop curriculum handbooks to assist teachers in relating the district curriculum and the textbook to the state standards. Furthermore, individual teachers such as Jin-Ah who are familiar with the curriculum can assist others in creating a quick reference document that aligns the curriculum with the textbook and assessment. Figure 4.4 provides a one-page format for aligning curriculum objectives with the state standards and appropriate textbook references.

FIGURE 4.3
Overall Time Use in Classroom

Observer Simone Carter   **Date** 10/19   **Start time** 11:25 am

Teacher Jin-Ah Ko   **Number of Students** 31

Note only major activities (e.g. math lesson, reading groups, recess, etc.), but record all major changes in activities.

Start Times	Major activity for students in class
11:45	Enter class, get out homework, start a "sponge" activity that is written on the board (the sponge activity is a quick response item related to the lesson)
11:50	Waiting for Ms. Ko to check their homework . . . some students still working on the sponge activity
11:53	Talk about the sponge activity
11:55	Reviewed homework, asked if there were any questions . . . there was one
12:00	Listen and took notes on a lecture about mitosis
12:25	Talked quietly to each other (Ms. Ko told them to take the time for discussion since they couldn't leave for lunch for 5 more minutes)
	NOTE: the period is split in half with a 30-minute lunch break
1:00	Students start to arrive back from lunch
1:05	Students listen to lab instructions and review how to use a microscope
1:20	Students go to their lab stations, one person from each station comes to Ms. Ko to get an onion slide to observe mitosis
1:25	Students make observations using the microscope
1:42	Ms. Ko asks students to clean-up, hand in their drawings, and return to their seats, encouraging them to hurry as the bell is about to ring
1:45	Bell rings, some students are still trying to clean up, others are leaving

◄
___

Reflect on the Teacher: Case 4A

- *How much of Jin-Ah's 90-minute instructional period was focused on instruction?*

- *Where was she losing time?*

- *How can she make better use of her time?*

- *This time-use chart reflects two separate lessons that Jin-Ah used before the school switched to block scheduling. How could she better integrate the two lessons to optimize the 90-minute block?*

FIGURE 4.4
Quick Reference to the Adopted Curriculum
Developed by Jin-Ah

State Standard Number	Curriculum Objective Statement	Textbook Chapters	Number of Questions on End-of-Course Assessment	Notes (Key Skills, Activities, Common Student Concerns)
	Students will investigate and understand . . .			
B.1	how to plan and conduct laboratory investigations	Pp. v–xi; Chapter 1	5	Text is only introductory; provide handouts on lab safety
B.2	knowledge of cellular biology as it applies to the life processes of plants and animals	Chapters 2–4	7	Pre-assess students on material from middle school life science and build
B.3	how chemical processes are necessary for life	Chapter 5	4	Role of key chemicals in growth of plants, importance of water
B.4	genetics	Chapters 6–8	7	Include fruit fly lab and Mendel simulation Student trouble spot is meiosis and mitosis . . . use supplemental sources
B.5	biological evolution including the concept of natural selection, why variation occurs, and Hardy-Weinberg equilibrium	Chapters 9–11	3	Tie into U.S. History in the 1920's with the Scopes Trial; use the Web site on Galapagos
B.6	the modern system for the classification of organisms	Chapters 15–26	8	Emphasis on animal kingdom
B.7	human physiology as the internal environment of the body remains homeostatic despite changes in the external environment	Chapters 27–31; 33–34	4	Use space travel as a hook; discuss implications of extreme external changes
B.8	organism response to disease	Chapter 32	2	American chestnut blight, dogwood anthracnose, human diseases—AIDS, cancer; Use old text Chapter 14 for other organisms besides humans
B.9	how ecosystems respond to fluctuations in populations, environmental changes, human actions	Chapters 12–14	5	Small group investigation at the park

Planning and Preparing for Instruction: Long-range Planning

Jin-Ah and her fellow biology teachers sat down at the beginning of the school year and developed a long-range plan. This plan allows for teacher flexibility in accommodating for the speed students learn, while providing a common pacing guide for the department. By developing the long-range plan as a group, new teachers benefit from the expertise of veteran teachers who are often familiar with the concepts and content that students acquire quickly, where they struggle, and how instructional units can be presented during the school calendar to minimize the disruptions to instruction introduced by holidays and the testing calendar. Because calendar dates change, the blocks represent instructional weeks.

Many school districts operate around 180 instructional days or 36 weeks. The first step in developing a long-range calendar is to indicate all school holidays and known events, such as test dates. From there, teachers can begin mapping out the time for instruction on various topics (see Figure 4.5).

Planning and Preparing for Instruction: Short-Term Planning

With the growth of the Internet, there are many resources available to teachers beyond traditional print materials. Figure 4.6 suggests some sources Jin-Ah might consult to prepare for her Genetics Unit. Effective teachers have a broad knowledge of what is available and incorporate the materials into their instructional plan.

There is no ideal or universally accepted way to plan a lesson; however, school leaders or individual teachers may choose to adopt a uniform format to ensure that similar information is being considered and provided. Figure 4.7 provides a one-page lesson plan format that Jin-Ah shared with a teacher she was mentoring. The lesson plan can be used to organize information and communicate what is expected to occur in the classroom. In the space next to each heading are guiding questions that teachers may consider when determining what to teach and how to present it in a lesson plan.

FIGURE 4.5

Long-range Planning Calendar for 10th-Grade Biology

**Reflect on the Teacher:
Case 4B**

• *What does this long-range planning document provide? What does it not provide?*

• *Examine the time allocated in the long-range lesson plan in Figure 4.5. How does it relate to the weight of assessment items on the end-of-course test in Figure 4.4?*

• *What does this relationship between the end-of-course test and the allocated instructional time indicate?*

• *What factors might cause the teacher to modify the instructional plan in actual implementation?*

Start of School Course Intro, Lab Safety; Expectations (B.1) **Week 1**	Biology concepts pre-assessment: Determine individual students' entry-level knowledge/skills **Week 2**	Labor Day Holiday Cell theory, Structures and Functions (B.2) **Week 3**	Cell Biology (B.2) **Week 4**
Chemical Processes (B.3) **Week 5**	Chemical Processes (B.3) **Week 6**	Cellular Processes (B.2; B.3) **Week 7**	Science Project Design—Topic & Question (B.1) **Week 8**
Workday—Friday Science Project Lit. Review (B.1) **Week 9**	Grades Due Genetics (B.4) Science Project Procedure due (B.1) **Week 10**	Professional Development Day (Student holiday) Genetics (B.4) **Week 11**	Genetics (B.4) **Week 12**
Genetics (B.4) Science Project Results Due (B.1) **Week 13**	Genetics (B.4) Science Project Conclusion and Abstract writing (B.1) **Week 14**	Science Project Oral Presentations; Science Project Report due (B.1) **Week 15**	Genetics—natural selection (B.4) **Week 16**
School Science Fair Review for mid-terms **Week 17**	Mid-terms—no regular classes; Workday—Friday; Grades Due **Week 18**	Holiday—Winter Break **Week 19**	Holiday—Winter Break **Week 20**
Evolution (B.5) **Week 21**	Holiday—Dr. King's Birthday Evolution (B.5) **Week 22**	School District Science Fair Physiology start (B.7) **Week 23**	Physiology (B.7) **Week 24**
Immune response to disease (B.8) **Week 25**	Classification—Introduction and Monera (B.6) **Week 26**	Classification Protists (B.6) **Week 27**	Classification Fungi (B.6) **Week 28**
Classification—Plants; Review Plant Structures and Processes (B.2; B.3; B.6) **Week 29**	Workday—Monday Grades Due State Writing Assessment Rev. animal cells (B.2); Classification—Animal—arthropods (B.6) **Week 30**	Regional Science Fair Classification—Animal—fish, amphibians, & reptiles (B.6) **Week 31**	Classification—Animal—birds & mammals (B.6) **Week 32**
No School—Spring Break **Week 33**	Ecosystems—quick overview (B.9) **Week 34**	Review for state test **Week 35**	State End-of-Course Test—Tuesday **Week 36**
State Science Fair Ecosystems—Small Group Projects (B.9) **Week 37**	Ecosystem—Small Group Projects (B.9) **Week 38**	Review for Exams or Independent Study **Week 39**	Last Week of School—Exams for students who did not pass state assessment; Workday—Friday Grades Due **Week 40**

FIGURE 4.6
Instructional Resources

Topic: Genetics

Directions: Use this sheet as an organizer for key resources that can be used as different topics are addressed during lesson planning or in class.

Resources in the School
List any items that need to be reserved for use during study on this topic (e.g., incubator, graphing calculators, outdoor classroom, class set of novels, multi-purpose room).

       Computer room for the web scavenger hunt on inherited diseases

Resources in the Classroom
List resources that are in your possession that specifically relate to this topic.

       Fruit fly kit

Print Resources
Include professional reference books, journal articles, and reading material that would be appropriate for students.

	For Student Use
Cartoon Guide to Genetics by Larry Gonick	X
The Human Genome by Carin Dennis and others	
Scientific American issues with "Exploring your destiny"	X
File folder of collected lesson plans and activities	

Web sites

Site Name	Web Address	Description
Genetic Lesson Plan Ideas	http://www.kumc.edu/gec/lessons.html	Web site links to everywhere
Genetic Science Learning Center	http://gslc.genetics.utah.edu/	Univ. of Utah site—has a mouse cloning simulation
Human Genome Project	http://www.ornl.gov/TechResources/ Human_Genome/project/about.html	Information on the project started in 1990

Speakers—Include their name, specific area of expertise, and contact information
       Ryan Graham, horse breeder—taught his daughter, Heather in 2002
       Presentation on the role of genetics in breeding race horses. Call Sunny Grove Farms

Possible Field Trip Sites
Zoo to learn about their endangered species breeding program

FIGURE 4.7

The Basic Lesson Plan

Topic	*What specific aspect of the unit will be my focus?* *How does this topic relate to the lessons before and after it?*
Class	*Who will be the students participating in this lesson?*
Date(s)	*How long will it take to teach this topic?*
State Standards	*What state standards are addressed by this lesson?* *What other state standards outside the subject area does this lesson plan address?* *For example, in Jin-Ah's class the oral presentation of the science project also relates to an English state standard on public speaking.*
Objectives	*What do students need to know by the end of this lesson to satisfy the curriculum requirements?* *What do I want students to know that will enhance their learning?* *What should students be able to do after this lesson?* *For example, one could follow this template:* *The students will (insert a verb) (insert the topic) and demonstrate this by (insert the assessment measure).*
Resources Needed	*What photocopies are needed?* *What materials need to be made, collected, or organized (media, lab materials, equipment, manipulatives, books, etc.)?*
Accommodations Needed	*What are the special needs of some of the students?* *How will I differentiate instruction for various ability students?* *What additional resources or support may I need?*
Activities to Engage Students (attach copies)	*What will be my warm-up activity to activate students' thinking?* *How does this topic relate to students' prior learning?* *Based on my knowledge of the students, what additional scaffolding do I need to provide for them to access this topic?* *What instructional strategies work well?* *What activities have worked well in the past?*
Assessment (including homework if applicable)	*What will enhance student understanding and learning?* *Are there related assignments in the textbook or on a photocopy sheet that can used for homework?* *How will I provide feedback to the students?*
Reflection	*What changes did I make during the lesson and why?* *How did I alter the lesson between the different periods I taught it?* *What needs to be done differently if this lesson is taught again?* *What worked well?*

Making Connections

Consider the Scenario

Reread the teacher scenario at the beginning of this chapter and review the information about Jin-Ah throughout the chapter. Consider the questions below.

Using the space provided, summarize what positive teacher behaviors and actions Jin-Ah displays, and what performance areas need improvement.

Positive Attributes	Areas for Improvement

What descriptor best describes Jin-Ah's skills in the area of organizing for instruction?

_____ Master: demonstrates the complexity of the quality resulting in a rich learning experience for students

_____ Professional: demonstrates the quality most of the time so there is a productive learning experience for students

_____ Apprentice: demonstrates the quality well-enough for learning to occur, but performance is inconsistent

_____ Undeveloped: demonstrates sub-par performance of the quality

Why did you select a particular descriptor?

How could Jin-Ah's performance be improved?

Reflecting on My Current Performance

Rate your performance on the qualities associated with organizing for instruction using the explanation of each major quality highlighted in the chapter.

	Undeveloped	Apprentice	Professional	Master
Focusing on Instruction				
Maximizing Instructional Time				
Expecting Students to Achieve				
Planning and Preparing for Instruction				

Reflection Learning Log

What do I better understand now after studying and reflecting on organizing for instruction?

What are next steps to improve my performance?

What resources (e.g., people and materials) are needed to enhance my teaching effectiveness?

Resources

The *Resources* section contains three items:

▲ An overview of block scheduling research,

▲ the *Authors' Perspective,* and

▲ *blackline masters* of forms that can be used to promote improvement and reflection on qualities of effective teachers.

Overview of Block Scheduling

Block scheduling has been used in U.S. schools since the 1950s. Initially introduced in elementary schools as a means to reduce class sizes, it is now used to increase the number of courses a student may take, lengthen class periods, decrease discipline referrals, and increase test scores. A number of studies and articles on the subject of block scheduling have been written in the past 50 years. The bulk of material up until the 1990s focused on different types of block schedules, with a few studies on the relationship between the type of schedule and student achievement. With the advent of the current accountability movement, more research is being conducted to determine the effects of block scheduling on student learning. The use of block scheduling is on the rise. For example, in North Carolina between 1992 and 1998 the number of schools using a block schedule rose from 1.6 percent to 73.6 percent (North Carolina Department of Public Instruction, 1999).

Block Scheduling Research

In general, large-scale studies focusing on the perceptions of block scheduling are positive, but studies examining the relationship between the schedule and student achievement have inconsistent findings. A North Carolina study used 316 schools and found that schools on block schedules that were in their first year of the new schedule did not statistically differ from schools on traditional schedules; however, schools on the block schedule overall had higher state test scores in the area of Algebra I (North Carolina Department of Public Instruction, 1999). Oregon researchers examined school scores by the number of years the block schedule was in effect, and they found slight improvement in scores in blocked schools over schools with traditional schedules by year three (Higham, Johnson, & Gorow, 1996.). Texas has also conducted a statewide study based on school schedule type, finding that of the 72.6 percent of tenth graders who passed the mathematics portion of state assessment, traditional eight-period days had the highest mean passing rate of (79 percent) versus the modified A/B schedule (78.2 percent) or the accelerated 4 x 4 block schedule (70 percent) (Texas Education Agency, 1999).

When individual schools are studied, the findings are inconsistent, ranging from finding no difference (Schroth & Dixon, 1996) to favoring traditional schedules (Cobb, Abate, & Baker, 1999; Veal & Schreiber, 1999; Wronkovich, Hess, & Robinson, 1997) to supporting block scheduling with higher achievement scores (Center for Applied Research and Education Improvement and College Education and Human Development, University of Minnesota, 1995; Cobb et al., 1999; Reid, 1994; Snyder, 1997). A recent study found that science achievement was higher for students in a block schedule (Lewis et al., 2003).

Professional Development Prior to Implementing the Block Schedule

Block scheduling introduces major changes in the school day. It requires students and teachers to change how they use their time. Key to the success of block scheduling is professional development to prepare teachers to use their time differently. Some schools that implement block schedules do so without staff development, and some teachers use the additional time for students to complete homework. To realize the benefits of an alternative schedule, educators need to maximize time use. Canady and Rettig (1995), who have done a great deal of writing on the development of various block schedule designs and the positive attributes associated with it, suggest, "We urge school personnel not to move to any form of block scheduling if teachers are not provided with a minimum of 5 and hopefully 10 days of staff development" (p. 205). Teachers need to break down the longer period into different activities (Schoenstein, 1994). Teachers indicate that they attempted at least one new strategy that they had not used before going to the block schedule (Staunton, 1997). Without staff development, teachers may not have the additional strategies that they need to adjust to the longer block of instructional time. For additional information on instructional strategies see Figure 5.9 (p. 150).

The longer periods lend themselves to teaching strategies such as cooperative learning, Paideia seminars, simulations, labs, hands-on algebra, and other interactive activities. Because many teachers have been in the classroom for many years, they benefit from staff development on how to make the transition from the lecture format to the more activity-driven classroom (Canady & Rettig, 1995). One study found that teachers with block schedules used cooperative learning more often than teachers in schools with traditional schedules (Staunton, 1997). Even experienced teachers reported feeling like novices with the introduction of the block schedule (Kramer, 1997). Thus, staff development that helps teachers learn new strategies and gives them opportunities to write lesson plans is vital to effective implementation.

Mathematics is one subject where teachers on block schedules report curriculum changes need to be made. Kramer (1997) states that mathematics curricula need to be "adapted to reduce redundancy between courses and cover fewer topics in more depth within each course. In addition, math instruction should probably be spread over more courses during each student's high school career" (p. 19). The concern is that with a reduced number of classes that are longer, too many concepts may be introduced at once and students will not have time to process the material. Math and French teachers reported that they had difficulty covering the equivalent amounts of material teaching in a block schedule as opposed to a traditional schedule (Kramer, 1997). One study found that teachers are covering less material in the block schedule, but in greater detail (Staunton, 1997). When considering the content taught, the issue of depth versus breadth is a challenge that teachers continue to struggle with in the block schedule.

With an increasing number of schools across the country adopting some form of alternative scheduling, it is important to emphasize the need to prepare educators. In North Carolina (a state with a high percentage of high schools that have adopted a block schedule) administrators emphasized staff development as a key to successful implementation (Kramer, 1997). Canady and Rettig (1995) are concerned that if teachers do not alter their classroom techniques when block scheduling is adopted, then "the promise of the block scheduling movement will die" (p. 205).

Reflect on the Teacher: Authors' Perspective

The *Reflect on the Teacher* questions are provided to encourage interactive and reflective reading and application of the *Handbook for Qualities of Effective Teachers*. In most cases there are no right or wrong answers. The *Authors' Perspective* is provided as one way to reflect on the information presented.

Reflect on the Teacher: Case 4A (see p. 107)

How much of Jin-Ah's 90-minute instructional period was focused on instruction?

Jin-Ah used 69 out of 90 minutes on instruction-related items (figure 4.3). In analyzing the major activities, it appears that the students did a lot during the 90-minute period, but when looking at how the minutes added up, there was some unused time.

Where was she losing time?

Jin-Ah lost approximately one fourth of her instructional time in transitions and downtime. Transitions are a necessary reality in a science lab situation, but there was other downtime that could have been better used. When her students had something to do, such as the sponge activity, they engaged in it, but when they finished at different rates, they had to wait for the teacher to finish checking the homework to continue. There were 5 instructional minutes lost before and after lunch for a total of 10 minutes in one period (just over 10 percent of her instructional time in the block period).

How can she make better use of her time?

The split instructional period is a challenge in that the class effectively has to start twice. However, Jin-Ah could use this to her advantage. The students started on the "sponge activity" immediately at the start of the period. If she would provide some sort of activity when the students first come back from lunch, then she could reclaim five minutes. In looking at Figure 4.3, the after-lunch "sponge activity" for students could have been collecting the necessary materials needed for the lab and reporting to their lab stations (this took five minutes of instructional time once class started).

Another place Jin-Ah could have made better use of her time was before lunch when she had finished her lecture and let students talk. She could have taken that time to review how to use a microscope and the related lab safety rules. The five minutes saved there would have given students more lab time so they would not have been so rushed at the end of the period.

Using various strategies for time efficiency such as those suggested above, Jin-Ah would have reclaimed 10 minutes of downtime for instructional time. She still has 11 minutes of "lost time." Can it be reclaimed? The reality is that every classroom, despite the best efforts of the best time managers, will have some downtime. In the case of this science classroom, three minutes were taken to clean up a lab (often this task takes longer). A few minutes were "lost" waiting for students to finish a task. The most difficult lost time to get back is due to school scheduling. If students' 30-minute lunch period starts at 12:30 and ends at 1:00 without travel time to the cafeteria built in, then something else has to give. In this case, it is the resumption of the science class after lunch.

How could she better integrate the two lessons to optimize the 90-minute block?

The lapsed time before and after lunch could be reflective of Jin-Ah's mental model of class being 47 minutes long versus 90 minutes long, although the intervening lunch period certainly contributes to this mindset. By reconceptualizing the lesson as a gestalt of "theory" (mitosis) and "practice" (lab on onion cells), Jin-Ah could better bridge the two components of the lesson during the five minutes of extra time before lunch so that students would be ready to go, and possibly drawn back to class in anticipation of the lab work to follow.

Reflect on the Teacher: Case 4B (see p. 110)

What does the long-range planning document provide? What does it not provide?

The long-range planning document allots general time blocks for pacing. It indicates when instructional units will be covered, and it references the state standards. However, it does not provide specific details of how instruction will be delivered.

Examine the time allocated in the long-range lesson plan in Figure 4.5. How does it relate to the weight of assessment items on the end-of-course test in Figure 4.4?

If you rank-order the state standards by the number of questions asked and calculate how many weeks are being spent on each state standard, you will notice that the instructional time spent, in most cases, is proportional to the weight of a given standard on the test (see Figure 4.8).

FIGURE 4.8
Relationship of End-of-Course Test Items to How Instructional Time Was Allocated

	Priority Ranking by Greatest to Least	
Ordinal Position	**Number of EOC Test Questions**	**Instructional Time Spent**
1	B.6	B.6
2	B.2*	B.1
3	B.4	B.2
4	B.1	B.4
5	B.9	B.3
6	B.3	B.9
7	B.7	B.7
8	B.5	B.5
9	B.8	B.8

*when the amount is the same, the cells are merged

What does this relationship between the end-of-course test and the allocated instructional time indicate?

Jin-Ah and the other biology teachers have made a concerted effort to prioritize instructional time based on the high-stakes state assessment that students need to pass. The state standard dealing with laboratory investigations moved up two spots, but it also contained skills that permeated the other state standards. It also should be noted that the teachers chose the standard relating to the ecosystem (B.9) to be reviewed before the state assessment and taught at a deeper level after the assessment was given. This choice may have been due in part to the fact that students begin their study of the environment very early in their school careers, and the teachers knew that adding key vocabulary and concepts in a compacted manner before the end-of-course test would be sufficient for mastery on the test.

What factors might cause the teacher to modify the instructional plan in actual implementation?

Obviously, many intervening factors can force a change between the plan and actual classroom implementation of the plan. For example, if a group of students comes to the biology class without the needed prerequisites for success, the students will be much better served if the teacher takes time to target those needy instructional areas before automatically moving on.* The more longe-range the plan (as in this example, a full academic year), the more likely that some key components of the plan will become distorted. In fact, it is desirable to continually monitor the plan in relation to instructional delivery and, more importantly, in relation to evidence of student mastery. After all, a plan is merely a blueprint for the process; it is not the final product. Student learning is the final product!

Blackline Masters

The following blackline masters can be photocopied and used in your school or district.

---

*See Walberg, 1984, for a useful description of why monitoring prerequisite skills is an important instructional approach.

Overall Time Use in Classroom

Observer _____ Date _____ Start time _____

Teacher _____ Number of Students _____

Note only major activities (e.g. math lesson, reading groups, recess, etc.), but record all major changes in activities.

Start & End Times	Major activity for students in class

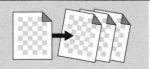

Quick Reference to the Adopted Curriculum

State Standard Number	Curriculum Objective Statement	Textbook Pages	Number of Questions on the End-of Course Assessment	Notes (Key Skills, Activities, Common Student Concerns)

Long-range Planning Calendar

Week 1	Week 2	Week 3	Week 4
Week 5	Week 6	Week 7	Week 8
Week 9	Week 10	Week 11	Week 12
Week 13	Week 14	Week 15	Week 16
Week 17	Week 18	Week 19	Week 20
Week 21	Week 22	Week 23	Week 24
Week 25	Week 26	Week 27	Week 28
Week 29	Week 30	Week 31	Week 32
Week 33	Week 34	Week 35	Week 36

Instructional Resources

Topic:_____

Directions: Use this sheet as an organizer of key resources that can be accessed as different topics are addressed during lesson planning or in class.

Resources in the School

List any items that need to be reserved for use during study on this topic (e.g., incubator, graphing calculators, outdoor classroom, computer room, class set of novels).

_____

_____

Resources in the Classroom

List resources that are in your possession that specifically relate to this topic.

_____

_____

Print Resources

Include professional reference books, journal articles, and reading material that would be appropriate for students.

	For Student Use

Web sites

Site Name	Web Address	Description

Speakers—Include their name, specific area of expertise, and contact information

_____

_____

Possible Field Trip Sites

_____

_____

The Basic Lesson Plan

Topic	
Class	
Date(s)	
State Standards	
Objectives	
Resources Needed	
Accommodations Needed	
Activities to Engage Students (attach copies)	
Assessment (including homework if applicable)	
Reflection	

IMPLEMENTING INSTRUCTION

Grace Fisher runs a well-organized classroom where students clearly are engaged in learning. At the end of the previous school year, the principal asked Grace if she would be willing to have a group of students identified as gifted assigned to her room, and she agreed. Unfortunately, the heterogeneously grouped classroom is not running smoothly and Grace is frustrated. She has tried to offer different learning options to her students, but all her preparation time seems wasted when she tries to teach. With many of her lessons, the lower-ability students don't get it, the gifted students quickly get it, and only the average kids seem to be okay. She does not want to draw attention to students by singling them out with special lessons. Nonetheless, she is about ready to just divide the fifth graders into ability groups and go from there.

Research Summary

The basic premise for an effective classroom is simple: teachers teach and learners learn. Thus, effective teachers engage students by meeting them where they are and taking them further. But as most educators know, nothing is ever that easy, especially when there is a classroom full of individuals with unique needs united by chance in a particular teacher's classroom. Grace is struggling with how to meet the needs of all of her students. Obviously, how she presents her lesson and what she expects of her students influences what the students will understand and be able to apply. Research on implementing instruction focuses on these factors:

▲ *Instructional strategies that work.* Research over the last 30-plus years has identified types of instructional strategies that are associated with increased student achievement. For example, a strategy called mastery learning can result in student achievement that is as much as one standard deviation higher than students taught without using this strategy (Bloom, 1984). Using strategies that work for different types of learners, such as hands-on learning that taps verbal, visual, and kinesthetic learners, has been shown to positively affect student learning (Wenglinsky, 2000).

▲ *Communication of content and skills knowledge.* Effective communication of content knowledge is a hallmark of good teachers (Ferguson & Womack, 1993; Peart & Campbell, 1999) and is associated with strong verbal ability, which was discussed as a prerequisite skill in Chapter 1.

▲ *Instructional complexity.* Students benefit from constructing meaning from the content while being supported by the teacher, especially when they are given opportunities to build on basic understanding and expand it into more complex, metacognitive thinking (Cunningham & Allington; 1999; Good & Brophy, 1997; Shellard & Protheroe, 2000; Wang, Haertel, & Walberg, 1993/1994: Zahorik, Halbach, Ehrle, & Molnar, 2003).

▲ *Questioning strategies.* Questioning strategies that emphasize higher-level thinking and student dialogue enhance student learning. Additionally, the proper use of questioning in instruction has a positive influence on young children's language development and analytical thinking skills (Martin, Sexton, & Gerlovich, 2001).

▲ *Student engagement.* Active involvement in the learning process is critical to student motivation and assimilation of new knowledge and skills (Covino & Iwanicki, 1996). The way a teacher instructs the class and the amount of individualized attention a student receives influence the teacher's effectiveness (Zahorik et al., 2003).

Figure 5.1 provides a visual overview of this chapter. Following an elaboration of the five key quality indicators associated with the quality of

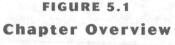

FIGURE 5.1
Chapter Overview

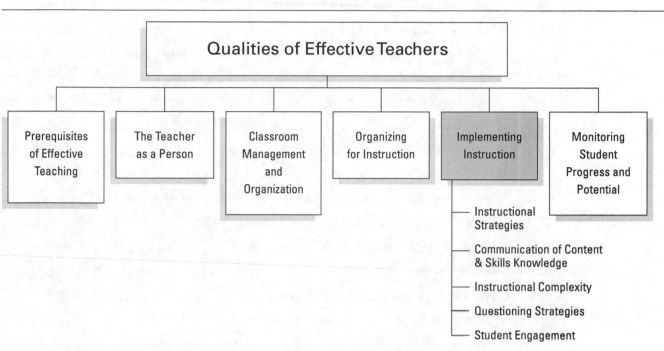

implementing instruction, tools to enhance effectiveness are presented in the context of our fictional teacher, Grace. The questions posed in the *Focus on the Teacher* section are addressed at the end of the chapter and are followed by the presentation of the blackline masters.

Instructional Strategies that Work

Different students will respond differently to the same instructional strategy. Most students, however, are receptive when teachers take risks and try new strategies. New approaches can be refreshing and stimulating for both teachers and students. While it would be ideal to offer each student customized instruction to optimize their learning potential, the reality is that it is not feasible in most educational settings. Consequently, teachers sometimes plan and use approaches that they like, that they know work, and with which they have had success in terms of student learning. Some teachers establish an instructional routine using the same strategies every day such as lecture with

Cornell note-taking*, round robin reading† in the textbook, and paper-pencil homework. Or perhaps the teacher runs a series of demonstrations and hands-on activities, but leaves little time for teacher explanation, student reflection, and questioning. Having a routine offers consistency; however, if students' learning needs are not being met by the strategies employed, then they are not benefiting from the educational experience. A balance between routines and novelty in classroom instructional practices surely makes the classroom more robust and dynamic.

Obviously, the strategies that a teacher selects influence student learning. Many researchers and authors have described instructional strategies that have a positive effect on student learning (See for example, Bloom, 1984; Johnson, 1997; Langer, 2001; Skrla, 2001; Wenglinsky, 2000). Most importantly, effective teachers use a variety of strategies as opposed to a single rigid approach. A research study on instruction in small classes found that it is not enough to reduce the number of students in a classroom; the teacher's practices and strategies must change as well to enhance student learning (Zahorik et al., 2003). A variety of strategies need to be used to keep students engaged (Darling-Hammond, 2001), address differential learning needs (Tomlinson, 1999), and keep the classroom experience fresh. Keep in mind the following strategies and guidelines:

▲ Cooperative learning is a strategy commonly used by effective teachers to involve students and enhance higher-order thinking skills (Shellard & Protheroe, 2000).

▲ Direct instruction is a tool used by effective teachers as they clearly explain content, model concepts, offer feedback, and build understanding (Zahorik et al., 2003).

▲ Researchers comparing mastery learning, one-on-one teaching, and conventional teaching found that receiving one-on-one instruction

---

*Cornell note-taking is a strategy where a piece of paper is divided in half with questions on the left and the answers on the right.

†Round robin reading involves students reading sections (often a paragraph or a page of a passage, book, etc.) aloud on a rotating basis.

increased achievement by approximately two standard deviations compared to conventional teaching, and that students in the mastery learning settings achieved one standard deviation higher than conventional classes (Bloom, 1984; Walker, 1998).

▲ Hands-on learning results in students achieving at higher levels than peers taught without manipulatives or simulations (Wenglinsky, 2000). Also, instructional strategies that use students' prior knowledge in an inquiry-based, hands-on format increases student learning (Covino & Iwanicki, 1996).

As noted earlier, effective teachers use a variety of instructional strategies because no one strategy is universally superior with all students (Darling-Hammond, 2001, Educational Review Office, 1998). Instructional approaches need to match the lesson's objectives and should provide opportunities for all learners. A description of selected strategies appears at the end of this chapter in the *Resources* section (Figure 5.8).

Integrating a new strategy into your teaching repertoire doesn't just happen. It is easiest to add a new strategy through guided practice based on the transfer of learning professional development model (Joyce & Showers, 1980). Additional sources of innovation for expanding one's repertoire of instructional strategies include books, professional development sessions, videotapes, professional education conferences, and coursework. Common instructional strategies promoted in many contemporary sources include cooperative learning, differentiated instruction, mastery learning, hands-on learning, problem solving, and concept mapping. Moreover, each strategy has many variations. Regardless of the instructional strategy that you are contemplating, a few simple guidelines may help with the selection process and implementation of the strategy:

1. Review the current research on the strategy to determine if it has a proven track record based on solid evidence. Consult independent, refereed publications as opposed to opinion (op-ed) literature or materials created and promoted by the developer of the strategy.

2. Learn about the instructional strategy and how to apply it in a classroom. Attend a workshop on the subject, read about it, talk to other

teachers, and preferably observe other educators who successfully use the strategy.

3. Start off slowly and build your comfort level by focusing on one strategy at a time.

4. Stick with it in the short term. Try a strategy in a lesson and reflect on how it went. If it didn't go as well as you hoped, don't discard it just yet; instead, try it again later with different students or in a new context. Many teachers abandon new practices prematurely due to their lack of comfort with a strategy. To avoid this understandable pitfall, get support from other teachers who use the strategy successfully and practice using the strategy until you also experience success with it.

5. Stick with it in the long term (but only if it works). Fresh approaches will enrich your teaching expertise and sense of efficacy. Also, expanding your repertoire of strategies will help you more effectively communicate content and skills to students and help build and sustain your students' interest in learning. However—and this is the critical issue in deciding whether to stick with a strategy —determine if it produces results. Evaluate students' performance with and without the new intervention. If students are better off with the new instructional approach, make it a permanent part of your repertoire; if not, discard it. The only reason to sustain any instructional practice is because it works.

6. Finally, continue to refine your use of the strategy until you become an expert. Once the basics are mastered, branching out to other strategies is a natural next step.

It is interesting and, given the focus on reducing class size in both public and private schools, especially pertinent to consider the impact of instructional strategies on student achievement in smaller classes. As one research team found, "class-size reduction alone doesn't always lead to high student performance; teachers must also acquire and practice effective teaching strategies" (Zahorik et al., 2003, p. 75). In particular, they noted that the following instructional strategies resulted in higher student achievement in small classes:

▲ Instructional orientation: Teachers stressed both academic learning and social skills development; the teachers also stressed both basic skills and critical thinking.

▲ Time allocation: Teachers gave higher priority to foundational academic goals related to benchmarks and standards then they gave secondary attention to higher-order personal and social goals.

▲ Direct instruction: In higher-achieving classrooms, instruction was teacher oriented in combination with activity-based learning. The teaching method was explicit, with step-by-step instructions (i.e., teachers provided clear directions, explained concepts, modeled procedures, led class practice, provided feedback, and used scaffolding for student understanding).

▲ Management style: Effective teachers emphasized structure in both student and lesson management.

▲ Lesson delivery: Effective teachers kept a brisk pace, with four or more types of activities typically included in one instructional segment (Zakorik et al., 2003).

Regardless of the size of a class, one point in the application of instructional strategies is clear: *one size doesn't fit all students*. To illustrate, one study of math and science classes found that both direct instruction and discovery learning can be effective (Weiss, Pasley, Smith, Banilower, & Heck, 2003). "We do our kids a disservice by choosing one pedagogy and using it all the time. . . . The problem is that most teachers are not using either approach effectively" said Weiss when discussing the study (Hoff, 2003, p.8). Good instructional strategies that are properly implemented are the foundation of good instruction.

Communication of Content and Skills Knowledge

Effective teachers communicate their high expectations of what students need to know and learn. Students need to understand what important concepts and relationships are to be learned as well as what they must do to be successful in the class (Johnson, 1997). Moreover, students respond favorably when the classroom environment is supportive and the teacher's explanations are clear. There is a place in the effective teacher's classroom for both one-way (i.e., teacher to students) and two-way (i.e., a dialogue) communication. Two-way communication is often overlooked as part of the teaching process, but it is a necessary part of the learning process because it provides students with an opportunity to formulate and express what they know, why it is important, how it relates to other knowledge, and what it means to them. Dialogue is one of the best vehicles for promoting higher-level thinking (Gamoran & Nystrand, 1992).

The writing of lesson objectives is an example of one-way communication used to establish high expectations. Many schools require teachers to write objectives on the board. Unfortunately, few teachers explain the objectives to students and even fewer write the objectives so that they are meaningful to students. Consider which objective listed below means the most to you:

A. Objective 6.9
B. Statistics and probability: students will graph data.
C. Students will demonstrate their understanding of statistics by determining the appropriate graph for the data, accurately graphing it, and offering a reasonable interpretation of the data.

All three objectives mean the same thing to the teacher, but if you were a student in that classroom, only the third one (Choice C) would tell you what you have to do to be successful.

Effective teachers not only communicate the facts and essential skills well, but they also show how the information is relevant to students' lives. Their deep understanding of the subject matter helps their planning and instructional delivery (Rowan, Chiang, & Miller, 1997). The teacher possesses a substantial knowledge about the content and curriculum, and knows how the material fits into the broader curriculum (Educational Review Office, 1998). Additionally, the effective teacher instructs students on the content within the larger context of the world, relating material to their day-to-day living as well as academic subjects (Bloom, 1984). By creating context for their lessons, teachers help students organize and remember information (Marzano,

Pickering, & McTighe, 1993). Effective teachers understand and communicate lessons in a way that weaves facts into a meaningful tapestry. They build upon prior knowledge and assist students in making the necessary connections to their existing understanding of the subject.

The overall process of teaching and learning is a dynamic, two-way communication process. As discussed earlier, talking with students is one way to become better acquainted and develop relationships that are crucial to effective instruction. Dialogue is also a means to better understand students' prior knowledge of a subject and how the subject relates to their areas of interest. Often questions are used by teachers to promote this type of dialogue. The more conversational the questions are in nature, the more likely they are to generate not only teacher-student interaction but also student-student discussion. This approach communicates a genuine interest in the exchange of information and has been found to increase both motivation and achievement (Good & Brophy, 1997).

Furthermore, listening to students' questions and comments is important because students are in a unique position to offer feedback on how they perceive the expectations for their own learning. Informally, you can reflect on your own clarity by thinking about a time you gave directions about an activity.

▲ Did students ask basic "nuts and bolts" type questions?

▲ Did students need you to explain the subject again?

▲ Did you have to redirect students during the activity?

▲ Did students know what to do during the lesson and after instruction?

▲ Did students learn what you had intended for them to learn, based on the work (or work products) you saw?

To capitalize on student-to-teacher communication opportunities for the purpose of improving instruction, ask students to give you feedback at the end of a unit, a marking period, or informally as they are leaving class. By asking for feedback, you are communicating to students that high standards for acquisition of new knowledge apply to *everyone*—including you. See the blackline masters at the end of this chapter for feedback forms you can use (pages 160–163).

Instructional Complexity

Instruction is like a kaleidoscope: it is made up of essential parts that, when combined, create new and exciting learning experiences. A kaleidoscope uses three reflective surfaces and some irregularly shaped colorful pieces sealed in a container that turns and is transparent on the ends. The components are uninteresting by themselves, but when they are assembled, people will look through the kaleidoscope and see something new every time. Effective teachers know that learning involves more than just memorizing facts; it means connecting facts into mental frameworks that have meaning and represent patterns in a given subject area. To create this deeper type of learning, teachers must infuse instruction with both facts and the skills to comprehend, apply, analyze, synthesize, and evaluate those facts.

First and foremost, teachers need to understand what knowledge, skills, and interests students bring to the classroom. All students are unique because of their individual strengths, weaknesses, and prior experiences. Effective teachers meet students where they are and move them forward with the appropriate level of challenge and support. These educators are able to raise the achievement levels for all groups of students in their classrooms by varying the complexity of instructional tasks (Wright, Horn, & Sanders, 1997). Remediation, skills-based instruction, and individualized instruction are commonly provided to students based on their individual needs (Shellard & Protheroe, 2000). Furthermore, students are able to learn advanced skills so long as they are provided concurrent support for addressing their weaker skills (Educational Research Service, 2000). Many strategies that promote critical thinking or creative problem solving for gifted and talented students can be used to raise the instructional complexity levels for all students.

Teachers help students construct knowledge in multiple and meaningful ways. Sometimes unfamiliar concepts are connected to familiar ones to generate new understandings or enhance a basic concept. Models, diagrams, movies, and experiments can also provide students with the necessary connections to make sense of complex information. Recognizing the essential components of content knowledge and the ways in which students can demonstrate their understanding of it is necessary to good teaching. Knowing what questions to ask to further students' understanding and assess where they are is another skill of effective teachers.

Questioning Strategies

Good teachers ask good questions that check for understanding of the basic facts, skills, or ideas in a lesson and then push students to think critically and creatively about what they have learned. Some educators think of questions according to Bloom's Taxonomy: knowledge, comprehension, application, analysis, synthesis, and evaluation. Others consider the cognitive process involved in answering the question. Regardless of how we choose to categorize classroom questions, a timely, thoughtful question is an excellent tool for instructional delivery.

Research suggests that the way a question is posed determines the response given. Effective teachers phrase questions to encourage students to use the desired level of thinking from basic recall to evaluation of an idea. The amount of wait time after a question is asked influences the number of students participating in the lesson and the level of active participation (Good & Brophy, 1997). While shorter wait times might be appropriate for basic recall questions, longer wait times are needed for higher-order questions. Effective teachers are competent in using multiple levels of questioning successfully (Covino & Iwanicki, 1996). Typically, the purpose of the lesson will guide the questions asked. A table in the *Resources* section (Figure 5.9) provides key words and ideas for relating different types of questions to the cognitive demands made of the students. When students are just learning a concept, the questioning should be focused more on recall and comprehension to build understanding of the foundation upon which students will eventually build in order to answer higher-level questions.

One study found that teachers with more subject matter knowledge tended to ask higher-level questions and engage students in more discussion opportunities using techniques such as redirection, prompting, and asking for clarification (Covino & Iwanicki, 1996). Studies have not shown conclusively what type of questions increase student achievement, but we do know that questioning is most effective when teachers plan in advance, when they align question difficulty and a student's cognitive ability, and when teachers give students feedback (Cotton, 2000; Good & Brophy, 1997; Tobin, 1980; Wang, Haertel, & Walberg, 1993).

Effective teachers not only query students, but also teach them how to ask questions well themselves. A classroom environment where students regularly discuss what they are learning and pose questions to one another will lead to increased interaction and articulation of ideas and opinions, and will enhance students' ability to communicate about the topic. Consequently, students are transformed from being passive to actively engaged learners. Open dialogue of this sort also encourages greater critical thinking and helps students learn to communicate (Good & Brophy, 1997).

Student Engagement

Time on task is directly correlated with student achievement, for obvious reasons. On-task students are involved in their learning; thus, effective teachers seek ways to enhance student involvement in class. Techniques to involve all students in the classroom include calling on them in a random order, actively engaging students in minds-on/hands-on experiences, and validating student responses (Bloom, 1984). Additionally, effective teachers encourage students to apply, interpret, and integrate class material into what they already know (Shellard & Protheroe, 2000). They not only motivate students to participate actively in their learning by relating content to what students are interested in, but they also get students to see the value in learning (Covino & Iwanicki, 1996). Because student involvement is essential in their learning, having information on students' interests and abilities is helpful in the creation of learning situations where student participation is enhanced.

While the ideal is to have 100 percent of students actively engaged in learning 100 percent of the time, the reality is that—even for the most effective teachers—this is not realistic. However, there is evidence that effective teachers do attend to student engagement and seek to minimize disruptions. For example, one study found that highly effective teachers had a disruptive event approximately once every two hours, whereas ineffective teachers in the same school district had a disruption approximately every 12 minutes

(Stronge, Tucker, & Ward, 2003). Clearly, teachers need to be cognizant of what they are doing and how it affects their students in terms of time on task. Effective teachers know that students who are interacting with the material and others in a constructive manner will learn more, and so they do everything possible to maximize instructional activities that promote high student engagement.

Visualizing the Quality

Figure 5.2 graphically represents the five major considerations in the process of implementing instruction. They are presented here as discrete entities for the purpose of understanding, but each of these five areas reflects a complex understanding of the teaching and learning dynamic and all of them are intertwined.

FIGURE 5.2
Visual Representation of Implementing Instruction (Example of Clustering)

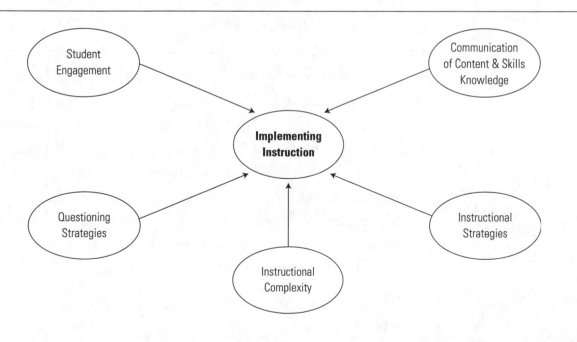

Focus on the Teacher

Grace is a caring, hardworking, and dedicated professional. Her principal identified her as a good teacher and asked her to challenge herself with the inclusion of the cluster of gifted students. The challenge is something Grace's principal knows she can meet. However, Grace needs support to critically analyze the instructional strategies she is using in the classroom to identify ways and means to address the problems she is experiencing.

A common challenge for many administrators and teacher leaders is how to help good teachers continue to get better. One strategy that is often over-looked is a systematic approach to supporting teacher self-assessment and reflection. Given Grace's experience and expertise, self-assessment is a perfect way of supporting her professional autonomy and desire to improve. Several specific exercises are suggested below. These activities are organized by the same key qualities addressed in this chapter. When a form is used, it is filled in with Grace's information. Consider the questions at the end of each section as you reflect on the teacher. The tools presented in this section of the chapter can be used to identify areas of strength and weakness to support growth in the proper selection and effective use of instructional strategies.

Evaluating Instructional Strategies

Grace has been teaching this year's class for several weeks now. There have been good lessons and lessons that could have been better. She feels that she uses a range of strategies. Instead of listing all the strategies Grace has incorporated in her teaching, someone suggested that she try categorizing them using the form in Figure 5.3 and her lesson plan book. Grace reviewed her lesson plans and placed a tally mark for each activity that she had used. Subsequently, she was able to see where she was spending the bulk of her instructional energies.

The next step would be for Grace to consider the match between what her instructional goals are and how she is addressing them in the classroom. She needs to think about questions such as the following:

▲ Did the strategies I selected enable students to learn the objectives I identified?

FIGURE 5.3

Sample from Grace Fisher's Lesson Plan Book on Strategies Used in a Unit on Statistics and Data Analysis (6th grade)

Categories*	Strategy	Tally	Total	Category Total
Identifying similarities and differences	Venn Diagram	/	1	1
Summarizing and note-taking	Note-taking	₳₳₳ ₳₳₳ //	12	12
Reinforcing effort and providing recognition	Test Review Game	/	1	1
Homework and practice	Practice problems from the text	/	1	4
	Independent practice	///	3	
Representing knowledge	Modeling	/	1	1
Learning groups	Cooperative learning	////	4	7
	Think, pair, share	//	2	
	Stations	/	1	
Setting objectives and providing feedback	Pre-Assessment (ungraded)	/	1	13
	Homework	₳₳₳ ////	9	
	Individual Quiz	/	1	
	Group Quiz	/	1	
	Test	/	1	
Generating and testing hypotheses	Inquiry	/	1	2
	Inferences	/	1	
Cues, questions, and advanced organizers	Concept Map	/	1	1

*Categories list taken from Marzano, R. J., Norford, J. S., Paynter, D. E., Pickering, D. J., & Gaddy, B. B. (2001). *A handbook for classroom instruction that works.* Alexandria, VA: Association for Supervision and Curriculum Development.

Reflect on the Teacher: Case 5A

- *Is there a pattern to Grace's instruction?*

- *Does one category of strategies dominate the instruction?*

- *Is a particular strategy over-represented?*

▲ Does my students' performance meet my expectations?

The role of reflection for effective teachers was discussed in Chapter 2, *The Teacher as a Person.* Reflection empowers educators to go beyond the first review of data to make changes where needed to improve their performance. In essence, all the forms used in this chapter are about taking this first step of reviewing current practice and creating an ongoing reflective dialogue, either with a colleague or alone.

Communication of Skills and Content Knowledge

Figure 5.4 shows a sample survey that Grace Fisher gave her students at the end of the unit. Grace's survey did not ask students *if* they had learned specific parts of the statistics and data analysis unit; she can determine student acquisition of knowledge based on her assessments. Rather, the survey focused on skills (questions 1–7), general content (questions 8, 13–14), communication (questions 10–11), and student perceptions (questions 9, 12, 15–16). She combined several aspects of high expectations by asking students to reflect upon their own work *and* her work. The percentage of student responses for each rating appears below the rating.

Instructional Objectives

A series of seemingly unrelated facts and skills is overwhelming, but teachers can help students make sense of them by offering students a finite number of strands to identify with an overall theme. Grace made a list of all the objectives she wanted students to master upon completion of a unit. Then, she cut the list apart and sorted the objectives into groups based on similarities. After the groups were established, she read the objectives and created a label for the group. In Grace's statistics unit she sorted the objectives into the following groups:

▲ representing data,

▲ talking about statistics,

▲ interpreting data, and

▲ misleading statistics.

FIGURE 5.4

Feedback Form on the Statistics and Data Analysis Unit

Below each rating you'll see the percentage of students who circled that number to answer the question.

Circle your level of agreement with each statement. Do not put your name on this paper.

		Low				High
1.	I listened to my study team.	1	2	3	4	5
		0%	30%	10%	55%	5%
2.	I stayed on task.	1	2	3	4	5
		0%	15%	50%	25%	10%
3.	I helped others.	1	2	3	4	5
		0%	0%	10%	70%	20%
4.	I offered my input.	1	2	3	4	5
		0%	50%	0%	25%	25%
5.	The team came to consensus (agreement)	1	2	3	4	5
		5%	5%	0%	55%	35%
6.	The team was focused on the work.	1	2	3	4	5
		0%	40%	0%	45%	15%
7.	Everyone participated on the team.	1	2	3	4	5
		30%	30%	0%	40%	0%
8.	Mrs. Fisher presented the material in a way I understood.	1	2	3	4	5
		0%	10%	0%	80%	10%
9.	The team work activities were fun.	1	2	3	4	5
		10%	10%	60%	10%	10%
10.	Mrs. Fisher gave clear directions.	1	2	3	4	5
		0%	0%	0%	90%	10%
11.	I knew what I needed to do to get a good grade.	1	2	3	4	5
		0%	20%	0%	70%	10%
12.	I learned a lot.	1	2	3	4	5
		15%	25%	0%	55%	5%

Answer the following questions. **Sample of responses is included.**

13. What was the best part of your study of statistics?
Finding out what my friends favorite things were (bar graph)
Figuring averages . . . now I know where grades come from
The M&M lab

14. What would have made the unit better?
Less group work
More time
Go faster

15. What did Mrs. Fisher do well?
Lots of cool things to sort and graph
Explained the box and whiskers graph so I got it
Nothing

16. What could Mrs. Fisher have done better?
Not review the stuff I learned last year
Make it fun
It was all good

Reflect on the Teacher: Case 5B

- *What did Grace's students think that she did well according to the survey shown in Figure 5.4?*

- *What statements did Grace's students disagree with the most?*

- *What patterns do you detect in the students' responses and what led you to identify those patterns?*

Everything done during the month-long study related to one of these four strands. Students could "file" the concepts and skills they were learning into one of these four strands. This sorting can be done in a very hands-on manner using large paper, scissors, and glue to help teachers and students conceptualize how all the parts fit together.

A visual approach that helps students focus on the essential elements of a lesson is the pyramid of knowledge. Obviously, students learn at different rates and retain varying amounts of information. The pyramid of knowledge (Figure 5.5) places the essential concepts that all students should know at the bottom or base. The next layer represents the skills that need to be developed

FIGURE 5.5

Pyramid of Knowledge for Grace's Instructional Unit on Statistics

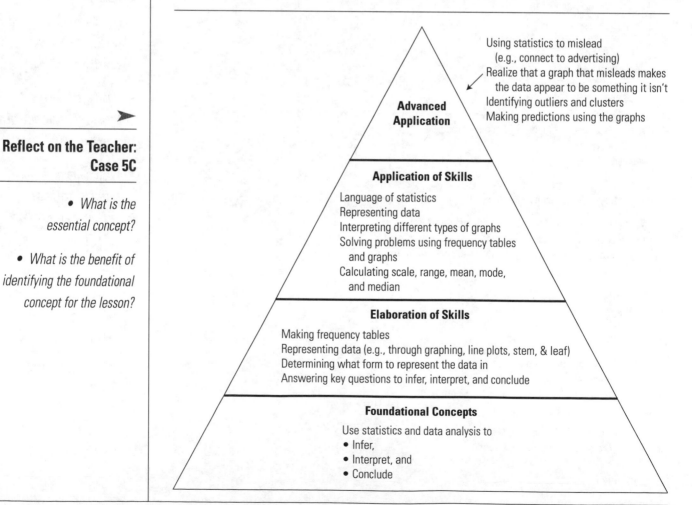

➤

Reflect on the Teacher: Case 5C

• *What is the essential concept?*

• *What is the benefit of identifying the foundational concept for the lesson?*

to enhance the use and understanding of the concepts. This level of understanding is followed by the layer representing application of the skills. And, finally, the top of the pyramid contains advanced application skills. This approach to thinking about what students need to learn clearly prioritizes concepts and skills for instruction.

Questioning Techniques

Figure 5.6 is a questioning techniques analysis chart using Bloom's taxonomy that asks an observer to classify and record all the questions asked by the teacher as recall questions, comprehension questions, or questions requiring higher-order thinking.

Grace may find it helpful to write down six to eight key questions to ask during a lesson. These questions should be concise and direct. By identifying a few key questions in advance, she can better target the cognitive levels she wants students to reach, and she can better ensure that she actually asks the questions in a way that will lead students to think in ways that she intends.

Increasing Student Engagement

Grace knows that most of her students are engaged during the lesson, but she has trouble keeping all of them focused. The student engagement graph and accompanying activity list (Figure 5.7) provide a visual representation of the highs and lows of student engagement during a specified time period. The combination instrument is used to sample student engagement every five minutes. Beneath the graph is a record of the class activity at each five-minute interval. Of particular interest are the patterns of when student interest seems to peak or to wane. By knowing what engages or "loses" students, Grace can adjust her practices to maintain higher levels of student engagement, resulting in higher levels of student achievement.

Charting student engagement is one way of providing valuable feedback to a colleague on the responsiveness of students to different instructional techniques. As with many instructional improvement tools, this captures only one point in time. Also, the presence of the observer may influence student behavior as may the day of the week, time of the class, content, and so forth.

FIGURE 5.6

Questioning Techniques Analysis Chart

Teacher's Name Mrs. Fisher   **Date** April 17th   **Time** Started/Ended 10:30 –11:35 am

Observer's Name Mrs. Clayburne   **Grade/Subject** 6th/Mathematics

Record all the questions asked by the teacher orally and in writing during the lesson. Place sample questions in the space beneath the appropriate level. Then tally the number of questions by level and calculate a percentage.

Type of Question	Total #	Percent
Recall How do you figure the mean? What is another word for mean? How do you calculate the mode? What is the median? The range? (2 questions) Where is the x-axis? What was being counted? How did we count?	16	38%
Comprehension What did you figure out was the average amount of time spent on HW? . . . watching TV? . . . sleeping? (3 questions) What activity do students spend the most time doing on average? What type of graph should be used here? What should the x-axis be labeled? What should we label the y-axis as? Title?	16	38%
Application and beyond (analysis, synthesis, evaluation) Why is the bar graph the best choice? What does the graph tell us? If you had to make a prediction about how another 6th grade class spent their time what would you say? What does the data tell us that the graph doesn't show? What is the advantage of graphing this data?	10	24%
Total of all questions	42	100%

However, the chart is useful for starting a dialogue about what is occurring in the classroom and how attentive and involved the students appear to be during the lesson. It is unlikely that 100 percent of the students will be engaged throughout the whole lesson.

Reflect on the Teacher: Case 5D

- *Based on the percentages reflected in Figure 5.6, what level of thinking was targeted?*

- *Did the distribution of questions reflect the lesson objective to make predictions using graphs?*

FIGURE 5.7

Mrs. Fisher's Student Engagement During a Lesson on Ranges, Scales, and Intervals

Start time: 10 am   **End time:** 10:48 am   **Date of observation:** April 14th   **Observer:** Mrs. Clayburne

Number of students in the class: Males 12 Females 15 Total 27   **Subject:** Math   **Teacher:** Mrs. Fisher

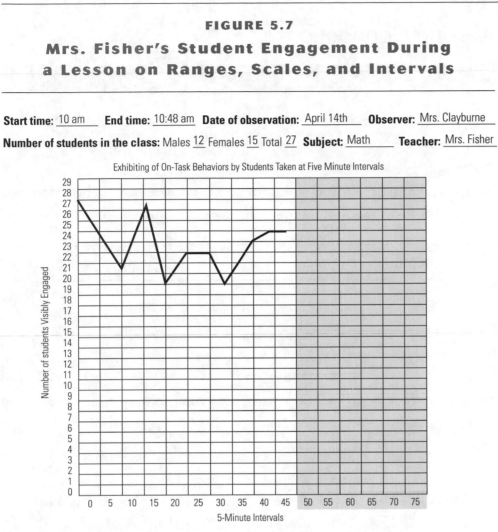

Class Activity during each interval:

0	Attendance, HW check-off, students getting materials out	40	Directions & Working in pairs
5	Addressed HW questions	45	Same
10	same	50	Session ended
15	Demonstrated range using 2 students; questions, some notes	55	
20	Note-taking, sample problem	60	
25	Guided practice with choral responses	65	
30	Independent practice	70	
35	Independent practice on range and interval, teacher checked off	75	

◄

Reflect on the Teacher: Case 5E

- *Looking at student engagement in Grace's class (Figure 5.7) and remembering her heterogeneous student population, what do you think is accounting for her dips in student engagement?*

- *What can she do to maintain student focus?*

Making Connections

Consider the Scenario

Reread the teacher scenario at the beginning of this chapter and the bits of information about Grace throughout the chapter. Consider the questions below.

Using the space provided, summarize the positive teacher behaviors and actions Grace exhibits and the areas she needs to work on.

Positive Attributes	Areas for Improvement

What descriptor best describes Grace's skills in the area of "implementing instruction"?

____ Master: demonstrates the complexity of the quality resulting in a rich learning experience for students

____ Professional: demonstrates the quality most of the time so there is a productive learning experience for students

____ Apprentice: demonstrates the quality well-enough for learning to occur, but performance is inconsistent

____ Undeveloped: demonstrates sub-par performance of the quality

Why did you select a particular descriptor?

How could Grace's performance be improved?

Reflecting on My Current Performance

Rate your performance on the qualities associated with implementing instruction using the explanation of each descriptor from the previous page.

	Undeveloped	Apprentice	Professional	Master
Instructional Strategies				
Communication of Content & Skills Knowledge				
Complexity of Instruction				
Questioning Strategies				
Student Engagement				

Reflection Learning Log

What do I better understand now after reading about the quality?

What are next steps to improve my performance?

What resources (e.g., people and materials) are needed to enhance my teaching effectiveness?

Resources

This section contains four items:

▲ a *table of instructional strategies referenced at the beginning of the chapter,*

▲ the *Guide for Classifying Questions by Cognitive Demand,*

▲ the *Authors' Perspective,* and

▲ *blackline masters* of forms that can be used to promote improvement and reflection on qualities of effective teachers.

Descriptions of Strategies

Descriptions of selected instructional strategies are presented in Figure 5.8. They are organized into the following categories: organizing and remembering information, learning together, investigating a problem, reading approaches, and writing and reflecting on a topic. These strategies are drawn from across the content areas and represent only a sampling of the options available for use in classrooms.

FIGURE 5.8

Instructional Strategies

Strategy	Description	Source for Additional Information
ORGANIZING AND REMEMBERING INFORMATION		
Graphic Organizers	Organizes information into a visual format such as a flow map, web, or Venn diagram. They provide a means for students to organize material visually and link ideas. For example, students may sketch out the process for the order of operations in a flow map showing what is done first, second, etc.	Clarke, 1990; Fisher, 2001; Fogarty, 2002; Hyerle,1996; Margulies, 1991
KWL Chart	Encourages the activation of prior knowledge by asking students individually or in a group to identify what they already *know* about a topic and what they *want* to know. Then after the learning activities on the topic asks the students to reflect on what they *learned*.	Wellington & Osborne, 2001
Mind Map	A visual tool to assist the student in remembering and associating key words and concepts. The key differences in this map from other graphic organizers are: 1) the connecting lines vary in thickness with main ideas being placed on thicker lines than words elaborating upon them and 2) each word has a picture beside it.	Buzan, 1991
Mnemonics	Assists students with remembering information. There are various specific methods such as the first letter strategy where the first letter of each word is represented (e.g., ROY G. BIV [red, orange, yellow, green, blue, indigo, and violet] for the colors in the rainbow).	Mastropieri & Scruggs, 1991

FIGURE 5.8

Instructional Strategies (continued)

Strategy	Description	Source for Additional Information
Odd One Out	Requires students to identify the word that does not belong with the others when given three words. Then the student tells why it does not belong (e.g., if given the fractions: 3/5, 1/2, 5/4 . . . which one does not belong? It would be the improper fraction 5/4 as the other two are proper fractions.).	Wellington & Osborne, 2001
Pyramid Learning	Organizes the information that students need to learn by a small number of concepts up top spreading out to a base of facts and skills at the bottom. It is used to help students conceptualize what they are learning. The same shape can be used to help students work from the bottom up to reorganize and reduce many facts into a few key concepts.	Watson & Houtz, 2002
Taxonomy of Words	Used to increase the awareness of specific word use in particular content areas by providing a framework for classifying words. Words are divided into four levels. The lowest level is *naming words* in which each word is tangible and observable. Level 2 contains process words describing something that happens. *Concept words,* level 3, represent ideas and are more abstract. Level 4 has *words* and *symbols* that are based in the theoretical and are meaningless unless the learner understands the underlying ideas.	Wellington & Osborne, 2001

LEARNING TOGETHER

Strategy	Description	Source for Additional Information
Fishbowl	Provides opportunities for students to respond to questions through a setup where a small group of students sits in a circle within a larger circle of their classmates. When the question is posed, the smaller group (fishbowl) is given an opportunity to answer. Students may rotate out of the fishbowl after a defined time or by exchanging places with someone on the outside circle who elaborated on a response by someone inside the circle.	Ysseldyke & Wiltse, n.d.
Human Graph	Uses students as points along a continuum to indicate their agreement with a particular statement. The leader tells students where to stand along an imaginary line if they strongly agree, agree, are neutral, disagree, or strongly disagree with the statement that is read. Then students can share their viewpoints.	Fogarty, 2002
Jigsaw	Allows students to become "experts" in an area and then teach it to others in the "home" group. A teacher divides students into groups in which each group learns something different and will be responsible for teaching their classmates. Then the teacher reassigns students so that there is one "expert" from each group in each newly formed group called a "home" group. Each member of the "home" group is an expert in a different area and responsible for teaching their "home" team members what they learned.	Aronson, 2000; Fogarty, 2002; Totten, 1995
Peer Tutoring	Provides an opportunity for students to help same-age peers learn a concept through one-on-one interaction in which the tutor provides support and feedback to the tutee.	Kalkowski, 1995
Socratic Questioning	Encourages students to refine their views and formulate explicit statements. The questions query students on their reasons for their assertions, how they are using terms, and problems that arise with using assumptions or faulty reasoning. The teacher and other students probe each other to generate a thoughtful dialogue.	Fogarty, 2002
STAD: Student Teams Achievement Division	Motivates students to support each other in mastering skills by offering team rewards. Students work together during and after the lesson, but take quizzes and tests separately. The mixed ability groups earn points based on their improvement and are recognized for their team's performance.	Slavin, 1995

FIGURE 5.8
Instructional Strategies (continued)

Strategy	Description	Source for Additional Information
Think, Pair, Share	Encourages students to *think* about a topic, and then *pair* to discuss with a partner before *sharing* their thoughts with the class/group. This is a means of involving all students in part of the class discussion.	Fogarty, 2002
Think-Aloud	Used to demonstrate what a thought process is. Teachers verbalize what they are thinking as they perform a particular task, read a passage, or solve a problem to enable students to hear the inferences and choices that are being made.	Readance, Bean, & Baldwin, 1989

INVESTIGATING A PROBLEM

3-2-1	Helps students discern between an inference and an observation. Think of the process in terms of a countdown: In step 3, students observe an event and record their observations. For step 2, they make inferences about what they saw. And finally, for step 1, they pose questions for what else can be investigated.	Thier & Daviss, 2002
4-Question Strategy	Used in science to determine what is available to conduct a study on a topic, what does the topic do, what can be changed, and what can be measured? Helps to form the foundation for designing an investigation.	Cothron, Giese, & Rezba, 1989
Creative Problem Solving	Facilitates decision making and problem solving. Students follow a multi-step process consisting of starting with a description of the issue, often called a "mess" or a "fuzzy problem." Students gather data about the issue, define the problem, think of possible solutions, evaluate solutions against criteria they developed and then test the ideas, and finally, reach acceptance where a plan of action is developed and implemented.	Isaksen & Treffinger, 1985
Discrepant Event	Use as a hook to get students investigating why something occurs. The teacher sets up a situation that motivates students to find out why it happened. Students are given an opportunity to investigate the event and try to figure it out by observing, recording data, and experimenting. Finally, they either resolve the event, or the teacher uses it as a departure point to lead the class in a discussion of what they know and what is occurring.	Carin & Bass, 1997; Friedl & Koontz, 2001
Experimental Design Diagram	Communicates the basic information about an experiment by focusing on the title, hypothesis, independent variable, findings, dependent variable, and constants. This rectangular diagram provides a consistent format for summarizing information from an experiment.	Cothron, Giese, & Rezba, 1989

READING APPROACHES

CLOZE	Assists students in using textual clues to fill in blanks in informational sentences. The teacher prepares a passage where key words are omitted (in the beginning one word may be missing from every couple of sentences). Students generate possible words to fill in the blank based on their knowledge of the text.	Dewitz, Carr, & Patberg, 1989
DARTS: Directed Activities for Reading Texts	Focuses students on key selections of text by having them sequence items, predict outcomes, or create diagrams. The teacher may modify a selection of the text (e.g., remove key words) so that students have to seek the information by examining a diagram to find the words they need.	Wellington & Osborne, 2001

FIGURE 5.8
Instructional Strategies (continued)

Strategy	Description	Source for Additional Information
DRTA: Directed Reading and Thinking Activity	Teaches ways to infer information and justify responses. Students predict what will happen, read, verify their predictions, and reevaluate their hypotheses.	Stauffer, 1969
Guided Imagery	Encourages students to use their imagination to understand text. The leader has students close their eyes and imagine with all their senses the scene that is described. This is used to help students construct a personal understanding of a topic that on its own may be too abstract or complex.	Thier & Daviss, 2002
Reading Frames	Uses a visual grid to organize information in which the categories or questions are listed down the side and examples or types run across the top. For example, the topic may be "graphs" the questions would be, "what does it looks like, when is it used, and how is it interpreted?" The types could be bar, circle, and line.	Royce & Wiley, 1996; Armbruster, 1991
Reciprocal Teaching/ Reading	Modeled by the teacher. This strategy lets students observe how someone comprehends an unfamiliar reading selection by formulating questions, clarifying, summarizing, and predicting. Then students can use the strategy to work in pairs or groups to read a selection together. During clarification time, students can ask their teammates about vocabulary words, ideas, etc. before summarizing the information. Finally, students predict what will occur next.	Thier & Daviss, 2002; Palinscar & Brown, 1986

WRITING AND REFLECTING ON A TOPIC

Strategy	Description	Source for Additional Information
Issues, Evidence, and You	Used as a writing response strategy, students read an article about an issue and *identify* the key issue(s). Then they seek *evidence* or facts and/or expert opinions that support the issue. Finally they offer their own opinion on the issue and its application to them (the *you*). Each one of these three components is addressed in a separate paragraph.	Thier & Daviss, 2002
Learning Logs	Encourage students to write about their experiences, questions, and reflections. It is a place to work out ideas and concepts. Students may write about what they think before the lesson, what they experienced or observed during the lesson, and what they now know or new questions that have arisen.	Santa & Havens, 1991
Semantic Feature Analysis	Helps students recognize similarities and differences in words. Teachers pick a category that students know and make a list of concepts/objects in that category. Then students decide what to explore about those items in a particular category. The objects are written in a column while the items to explore are in a row. Students should then indicate in the matrix if the object possesses each characteristic.	Pittelman, Heimlich, Berglund, & French, 1991
Word Alive	Encourages students to think about key vocabulary words by having them predict its meaning, look it up in the dictionary, rewrite the definition in their own words, identify synonyms and anonyms, sketch the word, and finally write a caption for the illustration of the word.	VDOE, 2001

Questioning

Figure 5.9 can be used to consider how questions can be phrased to target various levels of thinking.

FIGURE 5.9

Guide for Classifying Questions by Cognitive Demand

Type of Question	Teacher Generated (What does the teacher ask students to do?)	Student Generated
Low Cognitive Demand • Knowledge • Recall of information	Outline Recognize Recite from memory Identify Name Order Recall List Define	Procedural Questions: Can I do . . . What goes here? How do I . . .
Intermediate Cognitive Demand • Comprehension • Application	Discuss Classify Interpret Explain Create own meaning Predict Problem solving Demonstrate	Curiosity Questions: Relating to another topic Asking for more information Using information in another context Adding to teacher explanation with own
High Cognitive Demand • Analysis • Synthesis • Evaluation	Compare/Contrast Ask for cause/effect Ask about relationships between ideas/things Ask to differentiate Design or create (not copy) Plan Perform Predict outcome Evaluate/judge	Reflective Questions: What do you think happens . . . Why . . . What happens if . . .

Reflect on the Teacher: Authors' Perspective

The *Reflect on the Teacher* questions are provided in the chapter to encourage a more interactive and reflective reading and application of the *Handbook for Qualities of Effective Teachers*. In most cases there are no right or wrong answers. The *Authors' Perspective* is provided as one way to reflect on the information presented.

Reflect on the Teacher: Case 5A (see p. 141)

Is there a pattern to Grace's instruction?

Without seeing the lesson plan book, a pattern cannot be established for Grace Fisher. However, given the rather even distribution of the categories of summarizing and note-taking, learning groups, and setting objectives and providing feedback (in figure 5.3), we can infer that she probably uses these three strategies together.

Does one category of strategies dominate Grace's instruction?

Grace primarily uses strategies falling within three categories. However, the category of setting objectives and providing feedback is not only used the most, but also it has the most variety of approaches used in any of the categories. Based on her lesson plan book, we can surmise that she formally assesses students' progress on a continual basis.

Is a particular strategy over-represented?

Note-taking frequently is used. While other categories with multiple tally marks have a variety of strategies, Grace uses only one strategy within the category of summarizing and note-taking. There are multiple ways in which new content can be summarized that Grace does not use, but there is no indication that her approach to note-taking ever varies or is differentiated for student needs.

Reflect on the Teacher: Case 5B

What did Grace's students think that she did well according to the questions they rated on a scale of 1–5? (See figure 5.4, p. 143.)

The students thought that, overall, Grace presented the material in a way they understood (90 percent rated it a 4 or higher) and that she gave clear directions (100 percent rated it a 4 or higher). Most of the students "knew what I needed to do to get a good grade," so Grace clearly communicated her expectations to them; however, there were 20 percent of the students who did not agree with that statement.

What statements did Grace's students disagree with the most?

The students had mixed reactions on team-related activities. Statements they disagreed with included the following: offering input, staying focused, group participation, and how much they learned. Perhaps she needs to reconsider her use of group projects in this class. The critical issue is whether she can continue to use the group work while making the learning experience more robust on an individual student basis.

What patterns do you detect in the students' responses and what led you to identify those patterns?

From looking at the percentages of responses to each question and the sample of the written responses, there is a division within the class. The unit did not meet the needs of all students. Of particular interest are items where the student perceptions are split between high and low levels of agreement, such as in the case of question #4 where 50 percent said they did not offer input and 50 percent said they did. Some students may not feel comfortable and safe working in groups, depending on the team's make-up. Furthermore, students may need additional cooperative learning skills in order to take advantage of its benefits.

Reflect on the Teacher: Case 5C (see p. 144)

What is the essential concept?

Grace wants students to be able to use statistics and data analysis to read, interpret, and draw conclusions.

What is the benefit of identifying the foundational concept for the lesson?

The basics of vocabulary and mastery of different types of graphing are necessary to get students to the next level of understanding. The use of statistics requires higher-order thinking skills such as analysis, synthesis, and evaluation. Only by developing clarity around instructional objectives can Grace make the connection between basic knowledge and skills that provide the foundation for "essential concepts" and the higher-order skills. In the end, all students should complete the unit with a solid foundation. Depending on the learner, some will have a modest building atop the foundation and others will have a large structure. This approach to lesson design and application of instructional strategies offers a powerful opportunity to differentiate instruction and meet the learning needs of diverse students such as those that Grace has in her class.

Reflect on the Teacher: Case 5D (see p. 146)

Based on the percentages, what level of thinking was targeted?

The lower levels—comprehension and recall.

Did the questions' distribution reflect the lesson objective to make predictions using graphs?

No. Grace and the class spent more time reviewing the elements of the graph to construct it, indicating that some students needed more time to understand and execute the foundational concepts before moving on to the elaboration and application of skills. At this juncture, Grace might have considered allowing the students who understood how to construct the graph to complete some "challenge" activities that focused on skill-building while she worked more intensely with students who needed help with the basics.

Reflect on the Teacher: Case 5E (see p. 147)

Looking at student engagement in Grace's class and remembering her heterogeneous student population, what do you think is accounting for her dips in student engagement? What can she do to maintain student focus?

As can be seen with the chart, students lost interest during times when the teacher was addressing her attention to one or two students versus the whole group. When she engaged the whole group in choral responses or had them working in pairs, engagement was high. Clearly, more active assignment time (whether in the form of group work or student pairs) is effective with this group of students to maintain optimal attention.

Blackline Masters

The following blackline masters can be photocopied and used in your school or district.

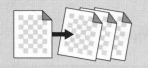

Record of Instructional Strategies Used

Categories*	Strategy	Tally	Total	Category Total
Identifying similarities and differences				
Summarizing and note-taking				
Reinforcing effort and providing recognition				
Homework and practice				
Representing knowledge				
Learning groups				
Setting objectives and providing feedback				
Generating and testing hypotheses				
Cues, questions, and advanced organizers				

*Categories list taken from Marzano, R. J., Norford, J. S., Paynter, D. E., Pickering, D. J., & Gaddy, B. B. (2001). *A handbook for classroom instruction that works.* Alexandria, VA: Association for Supervision and Curriculum Development.

Elementary School (K–2) Lesson Feedback

Directions: As your teacher reads the sentence color the face that shows what you think.

Example: I like ice cream.

---

1. I learned something new during the lesson on _____.

---

2. I did a good job working with others during the lesson.

---

3. My teacher gives me help when I need it.

---

4. I understood what my teacher wanted me to learn.

---

5. I am able to do the work in class.

---

6. I remember enough about the lesson that I can use what I learned again.

COMMENTS:

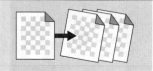

Elementary School (3–5) Student Feedback on the Unit

Directions: Follow along as your teacher reads the statements. Respond to the statements by placing a check mark (✓) beneath the response—"YES," "SOMETIMES," or "NO"—that best describes how you feel about the statement.

	YES	SOMETIMES	NO
EXAMPLE: I like going to the movies.	☑	❑	❑
1. My teacher listens to me.	❑	❑	❑
2. My teacher gives me help when I need it.	❑	❑	❑
3. I am able to do the work in class.	❑	❑	❑
4. I learn new things in my class.	❑	❑	❑
5. My teacher uses many ways to teach.	❑	❑	❑
6. I learned new information to remember.	❑	❑	❑
7. The unit was interesting.	❑	❑	❑
8. I can tell others what I learned from this unit.	❑	❑	❑
9. I understand the mistakes I made on some of my work during the unit.	❑	❑	❑
10. During group work, I helped others to learn.	❑	❑	❑
11. During group work, I participated.	❑	❑	❑

Tell 2 things you learned during the unit.

1.

2.

Tell 2 things you learned how to do during the unit.

1.

2.

What did you like best? Why?

What did you like least? How could it have been better?

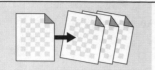

Middle School Student Feedback on the Unit

Do not put your name on this paper.

Circle your level of agreement with each statement.

		Low				High
1.	I listened to the team members.	1	2	3	4	5
2.	I stayed on task.	1	2	3	4	5
3.	I helped others.	1	2	3	4	5
4.	I offered my input.	1	2	3	4	5
5.	The team came to consensus (agreement).	1	2	3	4	5
6.	The team was focused on the work.	1	2	3	4	5
7.	Everyone participated on the team.	1	2	3	4	5
8.	The teacher gave clear directions.	1	2	3	4	5
9.	The teacher presented the material in a way I understood.	1	2	3	4	5
10.	The work activities for the team were fun.	1	2	3	4	5
11.	I knew what I needed to do to get a good grade.	1	2	3	4	5
12.	I learned new information.	1	2	3	4	5
13.	I learned how to use the new material.	1	2	3	4	5

Answer the following questions.

14. What was the best part of the unit?

15. What would have made the unit better?

16. What did the teacher do well?

17. What could your teacher have done better?

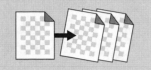

High School Student Feedback on the Unit

Do not put your name on this paper.

Subject _____ Period _____

Circle your level of agreement with each statement.

		Low				High
1.	I stayed on task.	1	2	3	4	5
2.	I helped others.	1	2	3	4	5
3.	I offered my input.	1	2	3	4	5
4.	Everyone participated on the team.	1	2	3	4	5
5.	The teacher gave clear directions.	1	2	3	4	5
6.	The teacher presented the material in a way I understood.	1	2	3	4	5
7.	The work activities for the team were fun.	1	2	3	4	5
8.	I understood how to do the assigned homework.	1	2	3	4	5
9.	The amount of homework assigned was reasonable.	1	2	3	4	5
10.	I knew what I needed to do to get a good grade.	1	2	3	4	5
11.	I learned new information.	1	2	3	4	5
12.	I understand how the new information relates to topics I previously have learned.	1	2	3	4	5
13.	I learned how to use the new material.	1	2	3	4	5

Answer the following questions.

14. What was the best part of the unit?

15. What would have made the unit better?

16. What do you still want to know?

17. How can you use what you learned in real-world applications?

Pyramid of Knowledge

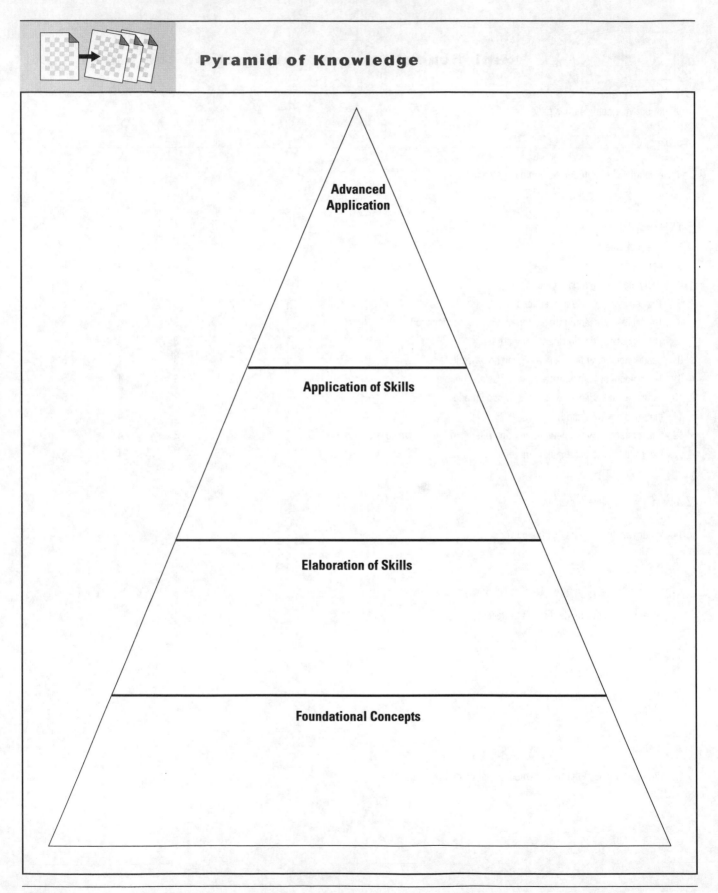

Advanced
Application

Application of Skills

Elaboration of Skills

Foundational Concepts

Questioning Techniques Analysis Chart

Teacher's Name _____ **Date** _____**Time Started/Ended**_____ / _____

Observer's Name_____ **Grade/Subject** _____ / _____

Record all the questions asked by the teacher orally and in writing during the lesson. Place a sample of the questions in the space beneath the appropriate level. Then tally the number of questions by level and calculate a percentage.

Type of Question	Total #	Percent
Recall		
Comprehension		
Application and beyond (analysis, synthesis, evaluation)		
Total of all questions		

Reflect

Based on the percentages what level of thinking was targeted?

Did the distribution of questions reflect the lesson objectives?

How clearly worded were the questions?

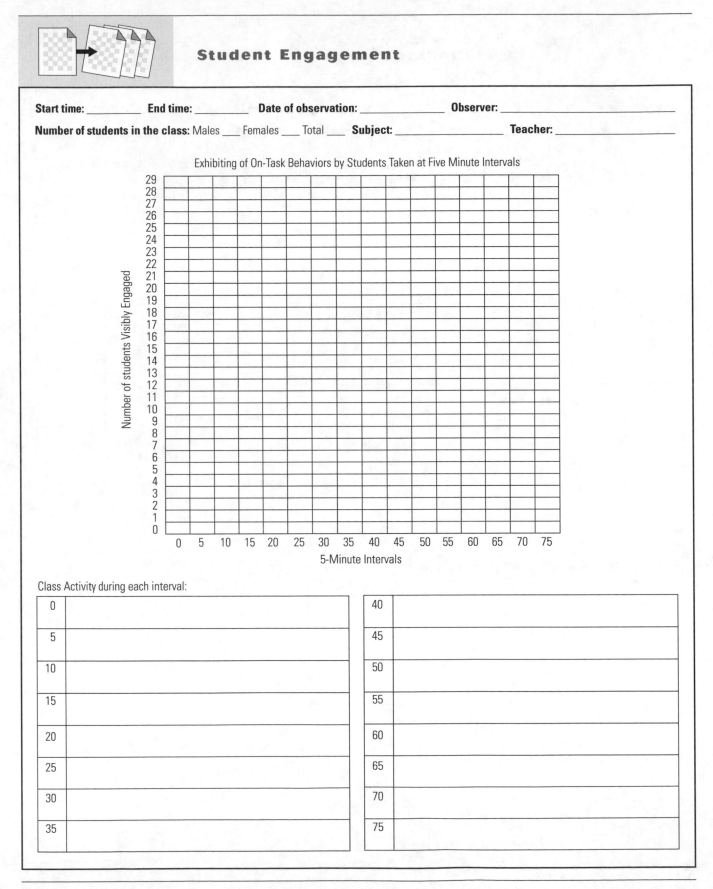

Student Engagement

Start time: _____ **End time:** _____ **Date of observation:** _____ **Observer:** _____

Number of students in the class: Males ___ Females ___ Total ___ **Subject:** _____ **Teacher:** _____

Exhibiting of On-Task Behaviors by Students Taken at Five Minute Intervals

Number of students Visibly Engaged (y-axis, 0–29)

5-Minute Intervals (x-axis, 0 5 10 15 20 25 30 35 40 45 50 55 60 65 70 75)

Class Activity during each interval:

0	
5	
10	
15	
20	
25	
30	
35	

40	
45	
50	
55	
60	
65	
70	
75	

MONITORING STUDENT PROGRESS AND POTENTIAL

Brandon Johnson has been teaching information technology for three years after retiring from a career in the military. As part of his role as a teacher, he plans, implements, and assesses his instruction. When observers learn that there are concerns about his grading practices they are always surprised, as the class functions as a well-oiled machine. Yet, each marking period, there are always calls from parents about students' information technology grades. Everyone seems to be under the impression that all is well, and then come the report cards and there are unexpected low grades.

Research Summary

Effective teachers do more than test students. They constantly monitor and collect evidence of student understanding. Research on successful schools indicates that one hallmark of those schools is that teachers use assessment to focus on student learning (Fullan, 2000). They make sure that students know what they are expected to know and design assessments to measure what students should know. Teachers use a whole range of assessment strategies, including informal means to check for student understanding (such as questioning, interpreting body language, and listening to the questions students ask) as well as more formal approaches such as testing. Both formative and summative assessment methods are employed, the former providing important feedback on the learning process for teachers and students and the latter offering comparative scores on the mastery of specific information.

Assessments are commonly used to evaluate a student's progress in learning new skills and knowledge. An assessment is "a formal attempt to determine students' status with respect to educational variables of interest" (Popham, 2002, p. 363). A broader perspective on assessment defines it as "the process of collecting, synthesizing, and interpreting information to aid in classroom decision-making" (Airasian, 1994, p. 266). The first definition focuses on assessment as a product, the second emphasizes assessment as a process. In fact, assessment should be a combination of both and should be tightly linked to instruction. Instruction and assessment are related in the following ways:

1. Directing instruction toward desired outcomes and the assessment of those outcomes;
2. Aligning instructional strategies and how they are assessed;
3. Differentiating instruction based on students' needs;
4. Using data-based decision making to guide teaching, inform assessment design, and review student performance on key knowledge and skills;
5. Keeping students informed of their progress; and
6. Targeting areas of strength and weakness to provide appropriate remediation (Gronlund, 2003).

Assessment is not merely giving grades. Rather, assessment provides feedback on how effective a teacher's instruction was in effecting student learning (Popham, 2002). It should serve as both guideposts along the path as well as endpoints to instruction.

In 1990, the American Federation of Teachers, the National Council on Measurement in Education, and the National Education Association developed the *Standards for Teacher Competence in Educational Assessment of Students* (as cited in Airasian, 1994). These seven standards (Figure 6.1) are skills that all teachers need to perform their professional responsibilities.

One challenge is that few states require assessment as a specific component in the licensure process (Stiggins, 2002). Therefore, many teachers have not had preservice or professional development opportunities to learn how to

FIGURE 6.1
Standards for Teacher Competence
in Educational Assessment of Students

Teachers should be skilled in:

1. choosing assessment methods appropriate for instructional decisions.

2. developing assessment methods appropriate for instructional decisions.

3. administering, scoring, and interpreting the results of both externally-produced and teacher-produced assessment methods.

4. using assessment results when making decisions about individual students, planning teaching, developing curriculum, and school improvement.

5. developing valid pupil grading procedures which use pupil assessment.

6. communicating assessment results to students, parents, other lay audiences, and other educators.

7. recognizing unethical, illegal, and otherwise inappropriate assessment methods and uses of assessment information.

Airasian, 1994

assess students in a valid and reliable manner or how to use the information they gain from assessment (Guskey, 2003). The seven standards in figure 6.1 describe what effective teachers do, although they were written for the larger audience of all teachers.

Monitoring student progress means that effective teachers continually interact with students to track student learning and adjust instruction as appropriate to meet student needs. Just as a physician tells patients their blood pressure and pulse rate, teachers keep students informed of their achievement. By knowing how the teacher perceives their acquisition of knowledge and skills, students can better respond to meet stated expectations. Families and other school personnel also need to be informed of students' progress and potential. Effective teacher research on this quality focuses on:

▲ *Homework.* Not only assigning homework but also providing feedback on it is a hallmark of effective teachers (Collinson, Killeavy, & Stephenson, 1999; Wenglinsky, 2000).

▲ *Monitoring Student Progress.* Effective teachers align their objectives, instruction, and assessments so that they can effectively facilitate student acquisition of knowledge and skills (Walker, 1998).

▲ *Responding to Student Needs and Abilities.* Differentiation does not occur just during instruction; it also influences assessment in terms of what types are used to measure student learning for different types of knowledge and skills or different levels of students (Tomlinson, 1999).

The above set of quality indicators for monitoring student progress and potential are depicted in Figure 6.2. Following an elaboration of the three indicators, tools to enhance effectiveness in this quality are presented in the context of our fictional teacher, Brandon. The questions posed in the *Focus on the Teacher* section are addressed at the end of the chapter, followed by the presentation of the blackline masters. By using both formative and summative assessments to drive instruction, educators have the potential to optimize student learning by making a wide variety of precision adjustments in pacing, content, and instructional activities. This potential is realized by effective teachers but is largely unrecognized by less-effective colleagues.

FIGURE 6.2
Chapter Overview

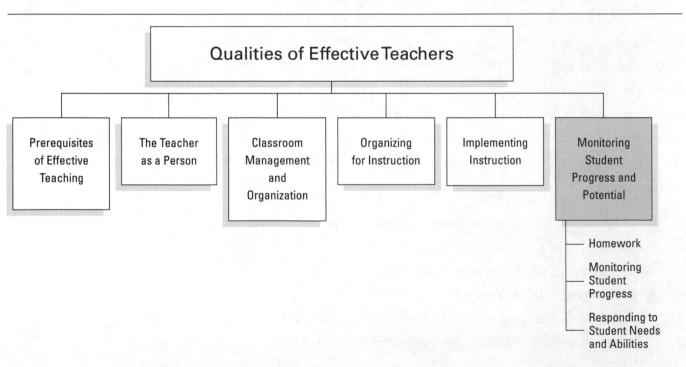

Homework

Making sure students and their families know homework expectations is beneficial to its successful completion. While teachers assign the homework, it is ultimately left up to the student and parent to decide when and where to complete it. One study with elementary students found parent involvement in homework to be predictive of students' grades (Cooper, Jackson, Nye, & Lindsay, 2001). For young students, parents can support their child in developing "good homework" habits, but teachers should not rely on parents to teach skills and content. Homework needs to be an assignment that students can complete independently and that is appropriate for being done outside the schoolroom (Danielson, 2002). Additionally, not all students have a supportive home environment for homework and teachers may need to suggest other options to students such as libraries, homework clubs, youth centers, and afterschool study halls or learning centers.

From classroom work to homework, effective teachers ensure that student work reflects what is taught in the class. These teachers carefully monitor learning activities to ensure that the tasks match the learning objectives and desired instructional outcomes (Cruickshank & Haefele, 2001). Homework may be used to reinforce a concept from the lesson, facilitate exploration of a related concept, or examine a topic in greater depth. Each of these purposes for homework presumes that the assignment is meaningful and supportive of the selected curriculum (Smith & Claxton, 2003). A positive relationship has been found between students' grades and the amount of homework they do (Cooper et al., 2001). However, it was not the mere completion of homework that enhanced grades, but rather the greater understanding of the material that resulted from completing the homework that made the difference. Effective teachers monitor student learning by checking homework and using it as a formative assessment to enhance student mastery of content material (Collinson et al., 1999; Covino & Iwanicki, 1996).

Sometimes teachers get in a rut when it comes to assigning homework. Consider for a moment how often the following events occur:

▲ math teachers assign practice problems;
▲ English teachers assign grammar exercises;

▲ history teachers assign chapters to read;

▲ science teachers assign vocabulary to define;

▲ physical education teachers do not assign homework;

▲ art teachers assign drawings; and

▲ _____ (you) assign _____ (fill in your own).

There is nothing inherently wrong with any of these assignments. Yet, homework can also be an opportunity for students to enhance their knowledge and skills through less traditional assignments (Corno, 2000). Physical education students, for example, could be assigned active homework such as engaging in physical activity outside of gym class and keeping a log of the activity and the time they spent doing it (Smith & Claxton, 2003). Students could watch the State of the Union address and participate in follow-up activities the next school day by discussing the political issues in history class and the use of persuasive speech in English class. Mathematics teachers working on area and perimeter in geometry could assign students to rearrange their rooms on graph paper. Service learning projects and academic challenges could be offered to students for more extended learning opportunities. The list of possibilities is limited only by our imagination.

Homework is also an opportunity for teachers to provide targeted feedback to students on their performance (Corno, 2000). Teachers may do this by using a rubric, in-class feedback, written comments, etc. These methods give students feedback that can be used to improve their performance in contrast to simply using a grade or a check mark that only conveys a judgment. The quality of the work produced by students should be used to determine how well students have learned the material and what difficulties or misunderstandings need to be addressed (Corno, 2000). By examining homework, teachers can gain valuable information about students and can also provide useful formative feedback to students.

Monitoring Student Progress

In many respects, the assessment process begins with instructional planning. Effective teachers define goals for their learners and monitor student progress towards those goals. The intended learning outcomes may be externally set (by state standards or by the district level curriculum, for example) but the effective teacher takes those goals and defines a path for students to follow in reaching the desired outcomes.

To monitor student progress, teachers must determine not only what their instructional goals are but also where students are relative to those goals. Teachers also need to understand the knowledge base and skill set of each student in order to set a realistic course for achieving goals (Airasian, 1994; Collinson et al., 1999). Teachers must be aware of the prerequisite skills needed to make progress and must be patient in letting students attain one level of skill or knowledge development before advancing to the next step (Covino & Iwanicki, 1996). Effective educators know their content area well and make every effort to present material in a manner that students can access and make their own (Airasian, 1994; Peart & Campbell, 1999). They use teacher-developed classroom assessment as part of the instructional process, resulting in more targeted instruction and higher levels of student performance when compared to students who are not so frequently assessed (Wenglinsky, 2000). Along the way, the teacher continues to monitor and adjust instruction to facilitate student acquisition of the defined goals using a variety of assignments and observations.

The role of quality feedback about student performance is substantial (Walberg, 1984). Effective teachers focus on providing feedback to students that enables the student to grow in knowledge and skills. Feedback is not limited to assessments on work submitted by students; rather, it includes the verbal and nonverbal exchanges that occur in the classroom. Effective teachers continuously check for student understanding during the lesson and adjust based on their observations and reactions from students (Guskey, 1996). Quality feedback provides students with information about their progress on the intended learning outcomes. Feedback is part of the ongoing dialogue between the teacher and the learner that informs both parties on the degree to which the intended learning outcomes have been attained. Effective teachers give regular feedback and reinforcement (Cotton, 2000).

Effective teachers are aware of the feedback they are giving and avoid showing preference to a particular student group (Bloom, 1984). Teachers work with students to help them determine what was done incorrectly and offer suggestions on how to improve so that the student is more successful in future attempts (Woolfolk-Hoy & Hoy, 2003). Effective educators know that specific (not vague or judgmental) feedback offered in a timely manner increases student achievement (Cotton, 2000; Marzano, Norford, Paynter, Pickering, & Gaddy, 2001; Walberg, 1984). When assessment is an interactive and constructive process between teachers and their students, student learning is enhanced.

Both formative and summative assessments offer opportunities for teachers to reflect on the effectiveness of their instruction and student learning (Wasserman, 1999). Formative assessments offer information about student learning during the instructional process while summative assessments are typically used at the end of the learning process. Analysis of both types of assessment can be particularly useful in setting future instructional goals (Cruickshank & Haefele, 2001; Gronlund, 2003). While traditionally there has been a heavier emphasis on summative assessment in education, it is the use of formative evaluation to inform instructional decision making that enhances student learning most dramatically.

Responding to Student Needs and Abilities

Every classroom is filled with students whose learning styles, needs, strengths, and abilities differ. Effective teachers do not see the class as one group assigned to a particular room, but rather as individuals (Tomlinson, 1999). After all, classes don't learn, students do—one person at a time. Educators need to consider how best to support each student's success. For some students, there may already be suggestions and support structures in place through Individual Education Plans (IEP) or Section 504 plans. These plans require teachers to make appropriate and specific accommodations for student learning. Sometimes a parent or student will mention a specific need (that a student is easily distracted and would benefit from a desk on an aisle, for example). Effective teachers adeptly address student needs and differentiate assignments for students at a higher rate than their ineffective counterparts (Stronge, Tucker, & Ward, 2003). Teachers learn how to make these accommodations from prior experiences, print and electronic resources, classes, and professional development offerings. For example, mathematics teachers who had a professional development course in working with students with disabilities learned to adapt their teaching in such a way that their students achieved at higher level than their peers (Wenglinsky, 2000). Differentiation is a means of optimizing education by making learning experiences engaging and meaningful for all types of learners through the modification of the learning environment, instructional strategies, assignments, materials, and assessments.

Differentiated instruction involves providing a variety of approaches and structures for learning. Creating positive classroom environments to support differentiation requires professional expertise, high expectations, connecting ideas and kids, energy, humor, and joy (Tomlinson, 1999). The teacher is a learner in this environment, identifying what is important in the subject matter, focusing on the goals of student growth and success, building on students' strengths, and considering the what, how, and why of learning (Tomlinson, 1999). Differentiation involves choices for students in terms of learning activities, special projects, and assessments. It also means accommodations for children with specific needs. Some students merely require subtle accommodations in what the teacher already is doing to be successful. For example, a student with fine motor control problems may need to have copies of the notes provided by the teacher or a classmate. Likewise, this student may need to tape record, dictate, or word process responses to essay questions as opposed to writing them freehand. Other accommodations need more planning and preparation on the part of the teacher, such as a student who must have all readings and handouts in Braille. Often, this means that teachers need to plan at least two weeks out to ensure that the Braille translator has the necessary materials ready in time. Differentiation can be done through the use of instructional strategies such as curriculum compacting, tiered activities, and cooperative learning (Tomlinson, 1999). Responding to students' needs does not mean that all instruction is differentiated, but it does mean that the teacher needs to stretch students by using a combination of approaches that mix traditional methods with new approaches (Burden & Byrd, 1994). In responding to student's needs and abilities, the responsive teacher is aware of the learner's preferences and considers students' needs and abilities in the planning, execution, and assessment of instruction.

Visualizing the Quality

The quality of monitoring student progress and potential focuses on three key quality indicators, two of which clearly overlap. Homework is one way of monitoring student progress and, as such, the two indicators are shown in a Venn Diagram (figure 6.3) with the overlap. Because teachers use multiple formative and summative assessments to determine student acquisition of content knowledge and skills, there is space left in the outer portions to recognize these contributions. Together, the first two indicators provide the information to the teacher on how to respond to students' needs and abilities, and is represented by the final circle.

Focus on the Teacher

Brandon Johnson came into teaching after serving in the Army as a captain. He was accustomed to strict discipline, clear expectations, and personal responsibility. He has established a sense of order in his classroom and his

FIGURE 6.3
Visual Representation of Monitoring Student Progress
(Example of Venn Diagram)

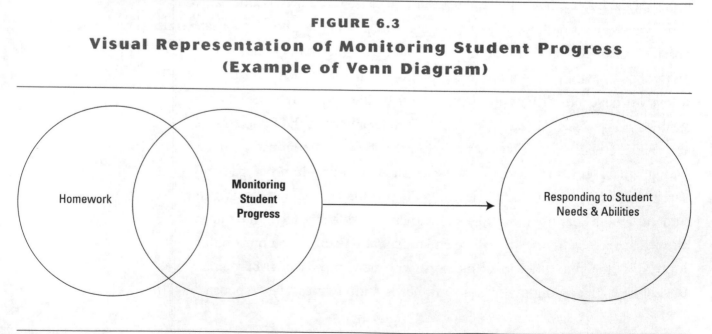

Homework

Monitoring Student Progress

Responding to Student Needs & Abilities

students know exactly how they are to behave. His teaching is "by the book" and he takes few risks in experimenting with different approaches to instruction or assessment.

Brandon's Use of Homework

Students in Brandon's class have a predictable routine when it comes to homework. Their families, for the most part, also know what to expect. During Back to School night, Brandon explained to parents his philosophy on homework. He followed up with a letter (Figure 6.4) that included the homework expectations. This letter also was sent home with students whose parents did not attend Back to School night. Thus, students coming to his 7th grade information technology class know what to expect. In holding students accountable for their work, Brandon is providing some extrinsic motivation in the form of grades as well as sending the message that homework is valued.

In the section on homework, we suggested that teachers sometimes repeatedly use the same type of assignments. Figure 6.5 suggests alternative homework assignments Brandon could use in his class.

Tracking Student Progress

Charla Campton, the assistant principal, observed Brandon's class one day when there was a class discussion about the growth of technology. She used a chart to record the level of student participation in the discussion. During a follow-up conversation on the observation, Ms. Campton asked what the goals were for the lesson and was told it was to discuss the development of technology from the late 20th century to the present. Brandon was asked how he knew if students had done the online scavenger hunt for information and the follow-up family interview to learn about the technology changes that were needed to participate in the discussion. He replied that he listened closely to the students and assigned a daily grade based on that recollection for the discussion. He added that he would review the family interview write-ups later. Then Ms. Campton asked if the students knew they were being

➤

Reflect on the Teacher: Case 6A

- *Review Brandon's expectations, homework, and grading policy information in Figure 6.4. What does he do well?*

- *What do you still want to know?*

FIGURE 6.4

Excerpt from Brandon Johnson's Back to School Night Letter

Class and Homework Expectations

It is expected that each student will come to class prepared to learn and contribute. Part of being prepared means that students will bring their books, writing materials, and completed assignments. Students are required to keep a notebook for the class that will be divided into sections based on the units studied. Within each section should be the daily objectives copied down by the student, homework assignments, classwork assignments, and notes. The notebook will be graded at the end of each unit for its completeness.

Homework Policy

I believe that homework is an important part of a student's learning. I also recognize that students and families have many demands on their time. My homework assignments generally require less than 30 minutes of work a night. If students find the assignments take longer than half an hour, I encourage them to speak with me individually. There are assignments that will take longer, but students also will have multiple nights to complete the assignment.

There are three standing assignments for students to complete each week that involve vocabulary building skills. Knowing this should help students plan their time in advance.

Wednesday night: Study for the vocabulary quiz using the words assigned the previous week.

Thursday night: Define or sketch the new vocabulary terms (10 per week).

Friday night: Write 10 sentences total using proper grammar and spelling for each of the vocabulary words.

Students will receive either graded or non-graded credit for every homework assignment they complete. For some assignments, students will receive credit for doing the work and other times they will receive grades based on the quality of the work.

Grading

There are three ways we will review assignments:

1. Self-correction: In class, students may ask questions about the assignment on items that they did not understand. I typically use this method when the answers are provided in the computer tutorial. Students receive full credit for completing the assignment on time and in the manner directed.
2. Peer feedback: Students edit each other's work to provide feedback and constructive criticism. Students receive full credit for completing the assignment on time as it was given and participating in the feedback process.
3. Teacher feedback: Most assignments are electronically submitted for review. Typically, I will return the work within two school days. The standing assignment of vocabulary definitions/sketches is an example of an assignment I grade to ensure that students have a basic understanding of the concept or term.

FIGURE 6.5

Alternative Homework Assignments
for Brandon's Computer Class

Instead of	Try	How
Vocabulary definitions in a list	Vocabulary Flash Cards	Write the word on one side and the definition on the other. In Mr. Johnson's case, the sentence could be added to the side with the definition.
	Vocabulary Reveal	Fold a piece of notebook paper so the right hand edge touches the red line before the margin where the holes are punched on the left. Unfold the paper and cut in from the right side to the crease every five lines. Fold the paper back. On the top of the flap write the vocabulary word. Unfold the flap and write the definition. Then students can quiz themselves as they learn the words. Works well in notebooks.
Writing correct vocabulary sentences	Breaking All the Grammar Rules	Have students write the vocabulary sentences where they deliberately break two to four grammar and spelling rules. An answer key can be written on the back of the paper. If specific grammar rules have been taught recently (need to coordinate with the English department), specify that students need to be sure to break those in a specified number of sentences. In class the next day, have students exchange papers and correct the mistakes. By looking at the answer key, Mr. Johnson could assess if students know the rules.

graded and how they would find out how they had done. Brandon did not have an adequate response for her. Ms. Campton suggested that Brandon try more concrete ways of recording students' interaction. She provided Brandon with a group discussion interaction chart (Figure 6.6).

Brandon uses a benchmark chart to keep track of when students meet specific performance goals. He wants to ensure that each student is computer literate on essential skills, while his ultimate goal is to have his students completely integrate computers into how they do most personal and academic tasks. Only the essential skills are noted on the benchmark chart. Students can attempt to pass the benchmark items as many times as it takes for them

➤

**Reflect on the Teacher:
Case 6B**

• *Summarize the student's participation*

• *What advantages and disadvantages are there to using a discussion chart?*

FIGURE 6.6

Student Discussion Chart

Date: 12/4   **Class:** 2nd period

Names of Students Who Are Absent: Melissa, Kenion, Lee

The first time a student contributes, write down the name. Indicate positive responses or contributions to the discussion with a plus sign (+) and incorrect or inappropriate responses with a minus sign (-). Mark each time a student contributes. Then provide an overall judgment.

Student's Name	Overall Performance	Response to: TQ	Response to: SQ	Asks Ques.	Adds Info	New Idea	Off-task
Samantha	[E] S N P	+	-	++	+++		
Remy	E S [N] P				+		
Curtis	[E] S N P		+			++++	
Cory	E S N [P]	-		-			- -
Valerie	E [S] N P	+			+		
Shaquita	[E] S N P	+		+	++		
Jessie	E S [N] P		+	-			
George	E [S] N P		++-				
Marc	E [S] N P				++		
Tamra	[E] S N P		+	+		+	
Alex	E [S] N P			+	+		
Laura	E [S] N P		+	+			-
Brad	E [S] N P	++					
Hee Suk	E [S] N P	++			-		
Amanda	E [S] N P		+		+		
Eileen	E S N [P]			-	-		
Madison	E S [N] P	+	-				
Jamison	E S [N] P				+		
Eddie*	E S [N] P	+				+	
Sarah	E [S] N P		+-		+		
Alonzo	E [S] N P		++				
	E S N P						
*answered TQ and	E S N P						
then in a follow-	E S N P						
up gave new info	E S N P						
	E S N P						
Did not talk	E S N P						
Tabitha**	E S [N] P						
Paul	E S N [P]						- - - -
	E S N P						
**watched and	E S N P						
appeared to be	E S N P						
listening	E S N P						

TQ = Teacher Question   SQ = Student Question
E = Excellent   S = Satisfactory   N = Needs Improvement   P = Poor

to demonstrate mastery. Students do not fail; rather, Brandon keeps track of the number of times a student attempts to pass the benchmark. On the chart, he notes the percentage of correct student responses when they attempted each benchmark (Figure 6.7). A benchmark chart encourages mastery learning by providing multiple opportunities to demonstrate a specific skill. Students are not given a failing grade for being unable to perform the skill, but instead are given another chance to do it correctly. This encourages persistence and full mastery of the basic skills identified.

FIGURE 6.7
Computer Benchmarks Chart for the Fall Semester

Student's Name	0%	20%	30%	40%	50%	60%	70%	80%	90%	100%
Identifies the parts of the computer										
Explains the parts of the computer										
Saves data to designated sources										
Retrieves data that is misplaced in one of the drives										
Demonstrates use of the virus scan program										
Transmits electronic messages and attachments										
Uses search strategies to find information										
Completes an original & edited word processed document										
Imports pictures into a document										
Formats a document given specific instructions										
Enters data accurately on a spreadsheet										
Uses formulas to calculate data										
Graphs the data										
Makes appropriate conclusions based on the analysis run										

80% is the minimum percentage to achieve a pass rating.

Another tool that is useful for reflection is the *Student Assessment Practices* (located in the resources section at the end of this chapter, p. 197). This tool is used to identify the types of assessments used in the classroom. An observer to the classroom can note what they saw and then engage in a dialogue with the teacher about assessment practices. An additional tool that can be helpful in designing useful and informative student assessments is the *Assessment Items Table,* also located at the end of this chapter, p. 199.

Accommodating Students' Needs

Brandon is able to respond to some students' needs without altering his instruction. For example, Lydia is a high-achieving student who has a degenerative eye disease. She can still see sharp contrasts, so black text on white paper or an overhead written with a blue or black marker enables her to access class material. Brandon does not use the chalkboard during the period she is in his class. Additionally, he has Lydia at a computer with a 19-inch screen and has adjusted the computer settings for a default enlarged view. However, there are additional students who need accommodations for their work. They may need more individualized attention, reinforcement, or time to complete assignments. Brandon also has students who are quite computer savvy. Brandon is meeting these needs by using computer software and individual contracting. The benchmark data discussed in the previous section is available in modules on the computer. For students who need more support learning the basics, their focus is on making the benchmarks. For the more computer-savvy students, they must demonstrate their competency in each area using the computer module tests before moving on to advanced applications of word processing and spreadsheets. Brandon uses a contract to individualize his instruction for the more computer literate students (Figure 6.8).

Academic Goal Setting

After the third-year review, Charla Campton, the assistant principal, suggested that Brandon use academic goal setting to focus his efforts on specific strategies to enhance students' understanding of their grades for the course.

FIGURE 6.8
Computer Learning Contract for Word Processing

Student's Name_____ **Date**_____

Having successfully completed all benchmark activities for computer literacy, you have earned the right to select your own projects. You may choose the order you want to pursue the items below. For each week of your contract, select an activity from a different row. In order to keep your right to choose your own work, you must complete one project a week for _____ weeks. In the event that you demonstrated competency early on the benchmarks, you may be entitled to renegotiate your contract at the end of this period.

Service to the Community	Serve as a peer tutor to a student (chosen by Mr. Johnson) and coach the student on the assignments given in class. Requires a training session outside of class time.	Word process submissions to the school's literary magazine, newsletter, or yearbook. You will be working for one of the sponsors for the activity listed above. Contingent on their need for services.	Create a brochure about the school complete with a labeled map (available on the class drive) to welcome new students to the building.
Extended Academic Option	Research and work on the required science project. You may word process components of your research paper.	Select a conflict in the world and write a paper on its origins, key people, current happenings, and implications for the future.	Research and write a biography about someone who contributed to a selected school subject. Suggestions include composers, scientists, writers, mathematicians, humanitarians, artists, etc.
Personal Option	Interview a family member about your family's history and write it up. Remember to edit and revise your work.	Write a technical piece explaining how to do a favorite activity. Include at least 3 pictures or graphics. Suggestions include skateboarding tricks, play three on three basketball, etc.	Write your autobiography in the form of a children's book. You will need to read samples of several children's biographies. Graphics should accompany the text.
Expand Creatively	Select a topic being covered in one of your classes. Get my approval. Then write the "cliff notes" version that contains the essential facts and explanations necessary for one to read your document and understand the concepts.	Create a bulletin board display highlighting a concept taught in class (in class display) or a happening in the school (displayed on the board in the hall). You need prior approval for the content from Mr. Johnson. Use word art.	This is a two-week activity.

Together they discussed possible goals and priorities given Brandon's efforts thus far in the area of monitoring student progress.

Commonly associated with teacher evaluation, academic goal setting focuses attention on instructional or program improvement through determining student baseline performance, developing strategies for improvement, and assessing the results. This process typically occurs through dialogue between the teacher and administrator about existing needs and how to prioritize efforts. Goal setting is intended to:

1) make a tangible connection between teaching and learning,
2) focus attention on student results, and
3) improve instructional practices and teacher performance.

Another purpose for goal setting is for personal improvement goals. In fact the same form shown here (Figure 6.9) was initially introduced for use in personal improvement in Chapter 1, *Prerequisites to Effective Teaching*.

Academic goal setting is *not* a means to make performance decisions based on results or to replace classroom observation and mentoring. Studies have found, however, that achievement gains in the range of 18 to 41 percentile points occurred when instructional goals were student centered, generally stated, and supported by the students (Marzano, Pickering, & Pollock, 2001). Academic goal setting is a formative way to raise student achievement by making use of available data such as standardized achievement tests, criterion-referenced tests, pre- and post-tests, end-of-unit tests, and other authentic performance measures (Black & William, 1998).

With input from Charla Campton, Brandon Johnson developed the annual goals shown in Figure 6.9 to address issues regarding the monitoring of student progress.

FIGURE 6.9
Teacher Annual Goal for Improving Student Achievement

Teacher _____ School_____

Grade/Subject_____ Administrator_____

School Year_____

Setting *[Describe the population and special learning circumstances.]*

The middle school has 900 students from an affluent area in a mid-size town. Most of the students come from highly educated families. Approximately 21% of the students participate in the free/reduced meal program. The Computer Technology class is an elective for 7th graders.

My 124 Computer Technology students represent the school population. I have 11 students who have special learning needs so I have to make specific accommodations for them in terms of class assignments.

Content Area *[The area/topic I will address (e.g., reading instruction, long division, problem solving).]*
Assessment of student work in InformationTechnology

Baseline Data *[Where I am now (i.e., status at beginning of year).]*

Student grades for the first marking period were the following: 33 As, 39 Bs, 28 Cs, 15 Ds, and 9 Fs. Despite regular feedback on the homework, students continue to make low grades and seem surprised by them at the end of the marking period. Some parents seem equally mystified.

Goal Statement *[What I want to accomplish this year (i.e., my desired results).]*

I will work to better inform students and parents about my grading system such that I will reduce complaints at the end of the marking periods for the rest of the year from 10 to 12 complaints to 3 or 4 complaints per marking period.

Strategies for Improvement *[Activities I will use to accomplish my goal.]*

- Meet with my mentor teacher or supervisor for assistance in developing detailed performance rubrics for individualized projects (learning contracts).
- Introduce the use of electronic software so that I can generate interim report cards for all students and more frequent reports if requested by parents.
  - Request the purchase of grading management software program by my principal
  - Attend a training workshop on how to use grading management software program
- Create a course syllabus that describes how I calculate the final grade for the marking period.

_____   _____
Administrator's Signature/Date   Teacher's Signature/Date

Reflect on the Teacher: Case 6C

- *Is Brandon's goal specific and measurable?*

- *Is the goal appropriate given what you know about Brandon?*

- *Are the strategies appropriate to achieve the stated goal?*

- *Do you think Brandon will be successful in achieving the goal?*

- *How will these strategies support the quality of monitoring student progress?*

- *How will these strategies enhance student achievement?*

FIGURE 6.9
Teacher Annual Goal for Improving Student Achievement (continued)

Midyear Data/Results *[What progress has been made.]*

Modifications *[Revisions needed to the strategies to accomplish the goal.]*

_____   _____
Administrator's Signature/Date   Teacher's Signature/Date

End-of-Year Data/Results *[Accomplishments by year end.]*

Considerations *[Thoughts, reflection on next steps for next year.]*

_____   _____
Administrator's Signature/Date   Teacher's Signature/Date

Adapted from *Handbook on Teacher Evaluation: Assessing and Improving Performance,* by Stronge, J. H., & Tucker, P. D. (2003). Larchmont, NY: Eye on Education.

Making Connections

Consider the Scenario

Reread the teacher scenario at the beginning of this chapter and the bits of information shared on the sample forms about Brandon. Consider the questions below.

Using the space below, summarize Brandon's positive attributes and the performance areas he needs improvement in.

Positive Attributes	Areas for Improvement

What descriptor best describes Brandon's teaching skills in the area of "monitoring student progress"?

____ Master: demonstrates the complexity of the quality resulting in a rich learning experience for students

____ Professional: demonstrates the quality most of the time so there is a productive learning experience for students

____ Apprentice: demonstrates the quality well-enough for learning to occur, but performance is inconsistent

____ Undeveloped: demonstrates sub-par performance of the quality

Why did you select a particular descriptor?

How could Brandon's performance be improved?

Reflecting on My Current Performance

Rate your own performance on the qualities associated with monitoring student progress and potential using the explanation of each major quality highlighted in the chapter.

	Undeveloped	Apprentice	Professional	Master
Homework				
Monitoring Student Progress				
Responding to Student Needs and Abilities				

Reflection Learning Log

What do I understand now after studying and reflecting upon the quality of monitoring student progress and potential?

What are next steps to improve my performance?

What resources (e.g., people and materials) are needed to enhance my teaching effectiveness?

Resources

This section contains two items: 1) the *Authors' Perspective* and 2) *blackline masters* of forms that can be used to promote improvement and reflection on qualities of effective teachers.

Reflect on the Teacher: Authors' Perspective

The *Reflect on the Teacher* questions are provided throughout the chapter to encourage interaction with the book. In most cases, there are no right or wrong answers. The *Authors' Perspective* is provided as one way to reflect on the information presented.

Reflect on the Teacher: Case 6A (see p. 178)

Review Mr. Johnson's expectations, homework, and grading policy information in Figure 6.4. What does he do well?

- ▲ Explains clearly what he expects.
- ▲ States how long homework should take.
- ▲ Encourages students to address concerns with him if homework is taking longer.
- ▲ Indicates that homework is valuable and demonstrates this by providing accountability in the grades.
- ▲ Tells how the grading is done.
- ▲ Tells when students can expect feedback on work that is submitted.
- ▲ Informs students and their families about "standing assignments."

What do you still want to know?

- ▲ How much are homework assignments worth in a student's overall grade?
- ▲ Are students responsible for making up homework if they are absent? If so, how long do they have to do it?
- ▲ What is the policy if the homework is not submitted by the next school day? Does Mr. Johnson accept late work?
- ▲ What criteria is he using to assess the work? Does he provide a rubric?

Reflect on the Teacher: Case 6B (see p. 180)

Summarize the students' participation.

▲ Four students were rated exceptional, three of whom were among the first six students who started contributing. They may have had more time to get points. Based on the observation data, we do not know if they made their points early in the discussion or if they were sprinkled throughout.

▲ Ten students participated satisfactorily. Their contributions were fairly evenly distributed.

▲ Five students were rated as needs improvement, three of whom participated late in the discussion as evidenced by when their names appear. It is possible to infer that they realized that the discussion was nearing its end and they had not contributed and knew that they should.

▲ Three students were rated poor for low quality contributions and off-task behavior.

What advantages and disadvantages are there to using a discussion chart?

Advantages

▲ provides a basis for making decisions regarding a participation grade in the discussion

▲ shows how students contributed

▲ shows when students became actively involved in the discussion

Disadvantages

▲ subjective for 1) determining if a contribution was positive or negative and 2) how the overall rating was determined

▲ does not show if the teacher question responses were student or teacher initiated

▲ shows who spoke a lot, but not the distribution of their responses throughout the discussion

▲ does not indicate the cognitive level of the questions or the resulting dialogue

▲ can be time consuming

Reflect on the Teacher: Case 6C (see p. 185)

Is Brandon's goal specific and measurable?

▲ His goal is specific ("reduce complaints") and measurable ("from 10–12 to 3–4").

▲ On the other hand, it may be hard to capture the total number of complaints because they may go to different people in the building or central office.

Is the goal appropriate given what you know about Brandon?

▲ Brandon is undertaking a number of effective strategies. For example, he is differentiating instruction for students, so he gives every indication of being willing to do what is necessary to meet students' needs. Student and parent complaints about grades seems to be the primary concern based on what we know about Brandon.

Are the strategies appropriate to achieve the stated goal?

▲ Yes, they are in keeping with his interests in technology and a systems approach to his work. They also should help to make his grading more transparent to students and parents.

Do you think Brandon will be successful in achieving the goal?

▲ These strategies should address the immediate concerns regarding how grades are determined.

▲ There may be other issues that cause concerns which will surface, aside from his grading policies.

How will these strategies support the quality of monitoring student progress?

▲ Rubrics will provide greater guidance to students regarding assignment expectations.

▲ Rubrics will also help structure Brandon's feedback on student work so that it provides guidance for how to improve performance on other assignments.

▲ A grade management software program will provide immediate feedback on missing assignments and grade point averages so that students will know where they stand on a daily basis.

How will these strategies enhance student achievement?

▲ The rubrics will provide guidance and corrective feedback on student work, which has been found to be critical to student mastery of concepts and skills.

▲ A grade management software program will ensure that students know how they are progressing while there is still time to get additional assistance, make up work, or expend extra effort on the final assignments.

Blackline Masters

The following blackline masters can be photocopied and used in your school or district.

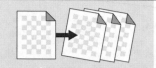

Student Discussion Chart

Date: _____**Class:** _____

Names of Students Who Are Absent: _____

The first time a student contributes, write down the name. Indicate positive responses or contributions to the discussion with a plus sign (+) and incorrect or inappropriate responses with a minus sign (-). Mark each time a student contributes. Then provide an overall judgment.

Student's Name	Overall Performance	Response to:		Asks Ques.	Adds Info	New Idea	Off-task
		TQ	SQ				
	E S N P						
	E S N P						
	E S N P						
	E S N P						
	E S N P						
	E S N P						
	E S N P						
	E S N P						
	E S N P						
	E S N P						
	E S N P						
	E S N P						
	E S N P						
	E S N P						
	E S N P						
	E S N P						
	E S N P						
	E S N P						
	E S N P						
	E S N P						
	E S N P						
	E S N P						
	E S N P						
	E S N P						
	E S N P						
	E S N P						
	E S N P						
	E S N P						
	E S N P						
	E S N P						
	E S N P						

TQ = Teacher Question   SQ = Student Question
E = Excellent   S = Satisfactory   N = Needs Improvement   P = Poor

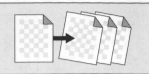

Benchmarks Chart

Directions: List the competencies that students need to know in order to demonstrate mastery of the topic being studied. Make sure that each item is clearly defined and measurable. Only one skill or knowledge component should be measured by each item.

Student's Name	0%	20%	30%	40%	50%	60%	70%	80%	90%	100%

80% is the minimum percentage to achieve a pass rating.

Teacher Annual Goal for Improving Student Achievement

Teacher _____ School _____

Grade/Subject _____ Administrator _____

School Year _____

Setting: *[Describe the population and special learning circumstances.]*

Baseline Data *[Where I am now (i.e., status at beginning of year).]*

Goal Statement *[What I want to accomplish this year (i.e., my desired results).]*

Strategies for Improvement *[Activities I will use to accomplish my goal.]*

_____   _____

Administrator's Signature/Date   Teacher's Signature/Date

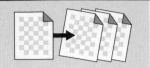

Teacher Annual Goal for Improving Student Achievement (continued)

Midyear Data/Results *[What progress has been made.]*

Modifications *[Revisions needed to the strategies to accomplish the goal.]*

_____   _____
Administrator's Signature/Date   Teacher's Signature/Date

End-of-Year Data/Results *[Accomplishments by year end.]*

Considerations *[Thoughts, reflection on next steps for next year.]*

_____   _____
Administrator's Signature/Date   Teacher's Signature/Date

Adapted from *Handbook on Teacher Evaluation: Assessing and Improving Performance,* by Stronge, J. H., & Tucker, P. D. (2003). Larchmont, NY: Eye on Education.

Student Assessment Practices

Observer:	Date:
Teacher:	
Grade/Subjects:	
School:	

Based on the classroom observation and your interview with the observed teacher, put a check in the columns opposite the indicated types of assessment that the teacher uses on a regular basis **for instructional purposes.** Please list any additional assessments used by the teacher under each category.

Type of Assessment	Observed	From Interview
1. Worksheets in Content Areas Reading Mathematics Science Social Studies Language Arts Other (specify)		
2. Commercial Workbooks Reading Mathematics Science Social Studies Language Arts Other (specify)		
3. Homework Assignments		
4. Oral Presentations/Reports		

Student Assessment Practices (continued)

Type of Assessment	Observed	From Interview
5. Hands-On Performance Computer Science Experiment Construction Project Dramatic Performances/Skits Chalkboard Work Art Project Classroom Displays Other (specify)		
6. Written Work Writing Journals/Folders Portfolios Other (specify)		
7. Teacher-Made Tests		
8. Prepared Tests (commercially prepared)		
9. Anecdotal Records Writing Journals/Folders Portfolios Other (specify)		
10. Other (specify)		

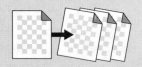

Assessment Items Table

Assessment Type	Item Type	Pro/Con	Writing Tips
Selected Response	True False	+ has only two outcomes + can have a large number of short items + easy to score - difficult to write beyond the knowledge level - reduces the probability of a wrong answer (favors student guessing) - results in no diagnostic information	Have a short statement Use precise words Write the statement with one central idea Place in random order
	Multiple Choice	+ asks for best or correct answer + measures most frequently comprehension and application - is vulnerable to poor construction and response selections - is possible for students to recognize a correct response that on their own they would not be able to generate	Clear language on the stem and the response Use parallel grammar Have appealing distracters that tap into students' misconceptions Use comparable length answers Emphasize negative wording so students do not miss a critical word
	Matching	+ reduces the space when the same set of answers would fit multiple question stems + reduces response time + easy to convert from a multiple choice question - difficult to identify items with the same response type - vulnerable to clues	Place responses in ABC order Use 10 or less stems for each set of responses Keep the responses and the stems on the same page Avoid excluding items (e.g., if Allies and Axis are in the same list a student could know one, but not the other and still get credit for both) Have more responses than stems
Supply Response	Fill in the Blank or Short Answer	+ easy to write and use + assesses knowledge well + relies on the student to generate the response - concerns with spelling or the use of synonyms - difficult to phrase for one correct response	State the question so only a brief response is needed Keep the response size consistent throughout Have one blank per question Place blanks at the end
	Essay	+ allows freedom of the response + encourages students to select the relevant information + measures the highest levels of learning outcomes + integrates and applies concepts - vulnerable to bluffing - takes a long time to score - has subjective scoring	Present a clear task Tell what is being measured Have all students write on the same set of questions Provide adequate time to write and suggest a time limit Use a rubric to score
Performance	Restricted	+ assesses oral and physical skills + combines knowledge and skills - requires more time - possesses low reliability	Identify the general objective desired, specific outcomes, and tell the measurable/observable dimensions Clearly state the outcome for students
	Extended	+ increases communication about the how and why + increases student participation - requires more time to perform and score	Should be feasible, developmentally appropriate, realistic, and meaningful

Adapted from Popham, 2002; Gronlund, 2003

EXPECTING AND GETTING THE BEST FROM OUR STUDENTS

Catherine's eyes shone in anticipation in late August, thinking of the students she would greet on the first day of school. Her teammate, Andrea, didn't share Catherine's enthusiasm, dreading the incoming class because of what she'd heard through the school grapevine. Fast-forward to the end of the first marking period: the two teammates are having very different experiences with the students they share. Catherine's classroom is humming with the sounds of engaged students; disruptions are a rare occurrence. Andrea, on the other hand, is constantly sending students out of the room, holding detentions, and writing referrals. It seems that each teacher experienced the proverbial "self-fulfilling prophecy."

Educators know that "high expectations" is a mantra for effective schools. Having high expectations for student behavior and achievement sounds great, but rhetoric isn't enough; teachers' actions must demonstrate that they believe in the power of expecting results.

So where do we go from here? In this brief concluding chapter we would like to refocus our attention on the purpose of the *Handbook for Qualities of Effective Teachers*: helping teachers like Catherine—and Andrea—become

This chapter is adapted (with permission) from: Hindman, J., Stronge, J., & Tucker, P. (2003). Raising the bar: Expecting—and getting—the best from your students. *Virginia Journal of Education, 97* (3), 7–10.

more effective with their students. In particular, we offer a few thoughts regarding:

- ▲ Expecting student success,
- ▲ Communicating high expectations for students,
- ▲ Striving for high expectations with all students,
- ▲ Focusing on the success of individual students, and
- ▲ Accepting responsibility for student success.

Expecting Student Success

Just as teaching is complex, so is the concept of student expectations. Effective teachers do indeed maintain high expectations for all of their students (Wharton-McDonald, Pressley, Hampston, 1998). Yet, holding high expectations is not a generic, one-size-fits-all concept. Rather, realistic expectations for student success describe the growth or improvement that individual students should make during the school year (Brown, 2002). A teacher may expect that all students complete assignments and contribute in class, but those expectations begin with early planning, continue with monitoring student performance, and then proceed with providing clear, concrete feedback to students.

Consider this: If Catherine plans with her students' needs and interests in mind, she is much more likely to enable them to connect new skills and knowledge to their prior learning (Fuchs, Fuchs, & Phillips, 1994). Additionally, she will better demonstrate that she values the students by incorporating their interests. By differentiating her instruction, she provides support that students need to be successful. Finally when Catherine offers feedback, even when it is corrective in nature, her students will be validated that they have learned the material and know what targeted items they still need to address. Catherine doesn't just pay lip service to a high-standards classroom; she models what high expectations mean in terms of what she does and wants from her students. Her approach would be a good model for her colleague, Andrea, and perhaps for any teacher hoping to improve the success of students.

Communicating High Expectations for Students

Teachers communicate not only a multitude of facts and skills, but also in a multitude of ways. Teachers need to clearly communicate their expectations to students. However, communication needs to be both one-way and two-way. When teachers use one-way communication, it is like a radio broadcast: Some listeners will tune in and others will tune out. One-way communication should be accompanied by two-way communication in which teachers talk with, not to, their students and their families. Effective teachers communicate by:

▲ using standard written and oral grammar;

▲ listening to the students and their families to refine and clarify expectations;

▲ making clear their expectations for learning (e.g., posting them in the room, sending them home to families, discussing them with students);

▲ offering clear explanations;

▲ involving students in the discussion of the expectations;

▲ providing opportunities for reinforcing the expectations;

▲ writing lesson objectives that tell what they will do;

▲ sharing these lesson objectives with students in such a way that the students will know how they are expected to demonstrate their knowledge and skills;

▲ modeling their expectations (Teachers need to model the expectations they hold for their students. For example, if Catherine says she values students being prepared to participate in the lesson, then she needs to have her materials prepared and deliver a well-prepared lesson.); and

▲ offering timely feedback to students and their families on how the students are meeting the expectations.

Striving for High Expectations with All Students

Good teachers would never assign students to groups and name one the "Soaring Eagles" and the other the "Common Blue Jays." Yet, researchers have found that the top students receive more attention and higher expectations from their teachers than students in the bottom third of their class (Good & Brophy, 1997). As with all of us, students need to feel important and valued. One key aspect of effective teachers is that they are perceived as caring about the success of their students (Peart & Campbell, 1999). Their caring needs to be felt by all the students in the classroom through encouragement, interest, and high expectations.

Two students may need very different levels of expectations, but they should have equitable support in achieving them. Note the word choice of *equitable*, not equal. Different students have different needs at different times. What is adequate for one may barely scratch the surface of needs for the other. Effective teachers support students striving to meet their learning expectations by:

▲ offering encouragement to all students at all levels of academic need;
▲ avoiding and eliminating biases and misconceptions when it comes to culture, ethnicity, or gender;
▲ seeing the differences in students as strengths, not liabilities;
▲ seeking opportunities for professional development that improve their work with student populations or subject areas that influence teachers' ability to support all students, and
▲ being aware of the power of the self-fulfilling prophecy.

Focusing on the Success of Individual Students

Students with disabilities are not the only ones who benefit from differentiated instruction (Tomlinson, 1999). Teachers with high expectations let *each* student know that they value good work and will do their part to ensure that students are provided with learning experiences that support students doing their best (Fuchs et al., 1994). These teachers believe in their ability to make a difference for every student. To that end, before they ever spend a minute in the classroom, they consider the class as a collection of individuals as opposed to one entity. This consideration starts before the first instructional minute is spent in the classroom. Effective teachers:

▲ make an effort to interact with students early in the school year with activities such as
  - telephoning students before school starts or mailing them a personalized postcard,
  - visiting students' homes early in the school year, and
  - providing opportunities for students to interact with each other and with the teacher to share their interests;
▲ analyze student data such as
  - reviewing cumulative records,
  - checking for gifted education plans, Individual Education Plans (IEPs), Section 504 plans, and medical alerts, and
  - looking for individual strengths and weaknesses (e.g., a student may have a good math score, but the sub-test shows a particular academic gap); and
▲ plan with students in mind by
  - considering students' interests,
  - providing support to remediate deficiencies while encouraging student learning,
  - incorporating different learning strategies that will stretch some students and allow others to shine, and
  - supporting learners' needs.

Accepting Responsibility for Student Success

Educators know that economics, family background, mobility, student ability, and a host of other factors influence student achievement. Nonetheless, we also know that what occurs in a school and in a teacher's classroom *is* within a teacher's realm of influence. Teachers' beliefs about their own ability and responsibility for student learning can have a dramatic effect on student learning. For example, setting expectations too high or too low can have a decidedly negative impact. Expectations must be realistically attainable and appropriate for the learner.

Many have heard of situations where teachers were told they had the "bright" kids who, in fact, were just "average," but because the teachers believed the students had higher intellectual abilities, they challenged them to excel and students did. More than a decade ago, researchers conducted a study of student expectations for 98 math teachers of more than 1,700 students and found that teacher expectations impacted achievement (Jussim & Eccles, 1992). Teachers who had high expectations for their students met with increased levels of success; conversely, those teachers who had low expectations for student performance experienced lower levels of achievement.

A decade later, a trio of writers asserted that teachers who accepted responsibility for student success were taking the first step that was followed by many successive steps aimed at promoting student learning (Corbett, Wilson, & Williams, 2002). They asserted that teachers who accepted responsibility for student success were taking the first step toward promoting that success. Furthermore, they suggested four ways in which teachers could demonstrate that they are responsible for student learning:

▲ *Have students complete all assignments.* If a teacher designed and assigned meaningful student work, then it should be done in order for students to learn. A "zero" is an easy out; instead of giving students zeroes, teachers should require students to do the work. This may mean having students come to class before or after school or during lunch. Corbett and colleagues interviewed students and found that, in general, students saw the value in the accountability and used it as one way of knowing if they were learning.

▲ *Require students to produce high-quality work.* The idea of effort and meeting a specified threshold for accomplishment is important in knowing if a student just tried the assignment versus understood the concepts in the assignment. A teacher may require students who receive a grade lower than a *C* on an assignment to come for additional help, rework the assignment, and receive additional feedback. Effective teachers show students examples of satisfactory work and of high-quality work. In this way students can evaluate their own products in addition to receiving teacher feedback. High-quality work is not the total burden of the student; rather, it is shared with the teacher who must make appropriate assignments and work with students as they struggle with challenging concepts and tasks.

▲ *Monitor student progress.* Effective teachers know how students are doing and, more importantly, are willing to help them. These teachers also can switch gears and present material in an alternative format to help students learn. They recognize when students are struggling and can troubleshoot the problem to help the student overcome it. Likewise, they are aware of students who may need acceleration as they learn quickly.

▲ *Go the extra mile.* Not all teachers can come early to school and stay after school to provide students with the extra help they need, but many do. This dedication is noteworthy and makes a difference for students. However, teachers can find other times to provide student support. Perhaps individual students can come in during lunch. Many secondary schools have homeroom periods where teachers can provide some one-on-one assistance. Another alternative is to carve out some time from the class, particularly if there is a small group of students who would benefit. The rest of the class could be furthering their own understanding while the teacher works with individual students off to the side. Finally, teachers may be able to use parents, school volunteers, or other community resources to provide extra support when given the specifics prepared by the teacher.

Teacher Success = Student Success

Expectation building is part vision and part promise. Andrea began the year with a "Let's see what they can do" attitude. In contrast, Catherine started off the year by telling her students that her overall goal was for them to walk into any science classroom and know how to approach a new problem. She wanted each of them to leave her classroom with the confidence and knowledge that they could achieve success. Catherine offered her students both a vision of what they could achieve and a personal promise to ensure their success. To fulfill her promise required significant work. Furthermore, she had to know her students in order to set appropriate and attainable expectations for them. While some expectations applied to the whole class, there were other expectations that targeted specific students. Catherine needed to carefully analyze data that she collected as part of her instruction and assessment to see how her students were progressing. She needed to adjust the level of assistance and support she provided depending on student learning. At times, she needed to be a strong motivating force for her students and, other times, cheer them on as they were driving themselves. While Andrea remained passive in her delivery of content and student assessment, Catherine actively pursued her promise of student success.

Establishing high expectations for students is not a simple matter and should not be approached with a one-size-fits-all mentality. When approached in the ways suggested above, it can be a powerful means of promoting high student achievement, but it clearly requires thoughtful and responsive planning, assessing, and teaching. In addition to the hard work, success requires authentic caring for students that is demonstrated through an investment in the potential of all students. Quality learning experiences for all students require quality teachers. In the final analysis, teacher success equals student success.

The *Handbook for Qualities of Effective Teachers* is aimed at helping all teachers improve their effectiveness and achieve success with their students. Throughout the *Handbook* we have attempted to offer "tools you can use" in the form of blackline masters to identify relative strengths and weaknesses in teaching ability, to support quality teaching where it exists, and to help improve teaching skills and results where they are needed. To these ends, we sincerely hope that this effort finds a fruitful place in your teaching practice.

REFERENCES

Airasian, P. W. (1994). *Assessment in the classroom.* New York: McGraw-Hill, Inc.

Allen, R. M., & Casbergue, R. M. (2000). *Impact of teachers' recall on their effectiveness in mentoring novice teachers: The unexpected prowess of the transitional stage in the continuum from novice to expert.* Presented at the American Educational Research Association, New Orleans, LA. (ERIC Document Reproduction Service No. ED441782.)

Armbruster, B. B. (1991). Framing: A technique for improving learning from science texts. In C. M. Santa & D. E. Alverman (Eds.). *Science learning: Processes and applications* (pp. 104–113). Newark, DE: International Reading Association.

Aronson, E. (2000). *Jigsaw classroom: History of the jigsaw.* Retrieved May 7, 2003, from http://jigsaw.org/history.htm.

Berliner, D. C. (1986). In pursuit of the expert pedagogue. *Educational Researcher, 15*(7), 5–13.

Betts, J. R., Rueben, K. S., & Dannenberg, A. (2000). *Equal resources, equal outcomes? The distribution of school resources and student achievement in California.* San Francisco: Public Policy Institute of California.

Black, P., & William, D. (1998). Inside the black box: Raising standards through classroom assessment. *Phi Delta Kappan, 80,* 139–148.

Blair, J. (2000). ETS study links effective teaching methods to test-score gains. *Education Week, 20*(8), 24.

Bloom, B. S. (1984). The search for methods of group instruction as effective as one-to-one tutoring. *Educational Leadership, 41*(8), 4–17.

Bransford, J. D., Brown, A. L., & Cocking, R. R. (Eds.). (1999). *How people learn: Brain, mind, experience, and school.* Washington, DC: National Academy Press.

Brophy, J., & Evertson, C. M. (1976). *Learning from teaching: A developmental perspective.* Needham Heights, MA: Allyn and Bacon.

Brown, D. F. (2002). *Becoming a successful urban teacher.* Portsmouth, NH: Heinemann.

Burden, P. R., & Byrd, D. M. (1994). *Methods for effective teaching.* Boston: Allyn and Bacon.

Buttram, J. L., & Waters, J. T. (1997). Improving America's schools through standards-based education. *Bulletin, 81*(590), 1–5.

Buzan, T. (1991). *Use both sides of your brain.* New York: Dutton.

Camphire, G. (2001). Are our teachers good enough? *SEDLetter, 13*(2). Retrieved November 12, 2001, from http://www.sedl.org/pubs/sedletter/v13n02/1.html.

Canady, R. L. and Rettig, M. D. (1995). *Block scheduling: A catalyst for change in high schools.* Princeton, NJ: Eye on Education.

Carin, A. A., & Bass, J. E. (1997). *Teaching science as inquiry.* Upper Saddle River, NJ: Merrill/Prentice Hall.

Cawelti, G. (1999). *Portraits of six benchmark schools: Diverse approaches to improving student achievement.* Arlington, VA: Educational Research Service.

Center for Applied Research and Educational Improvement and College of Education and Human Development, University of Minnesota. (1995) *Report study of the four-period schedule for Anoka-Hennepin district no. 11.* Retrieved September 9, 2000, from http://www.youthhandu.umn.edu/BlockScheduling/Resources/Research/REPORTs.htm.

Clarke, J. H. (1990). *Patterns of thinking: Integrated learning skills in content teaching.* Boston: Allyn & Bacon.

Cobb, R. B., Abate, S., & Baker, D. (1999) Effects on students of a 4x4 junior high school block scheduling program. *Education Policy Analysis Archives, 7*(3). Retrieved October 12, 2000, from http://epaa.asu.edu/epaa/v7n3.html.

Collinson, V., Killeavy, M., & Stephenson, H. J. (1999). Exemplary teachers: Practicing an ethic of care in England, Ireland, and the United States. *Journal for a Just and Caring Education, 5*(4), 349-366.

Columba, L. (2001). Daily classroom assessment. *Education, 22*(2), 372–374.

Cooper, H., Jackson, K., Nye, B., & Lindsay, J. J. (2001). A model of homework's influence on the performance evaluations of elementary students. *The Journal of Experimental Education, 69*(2), 181–191.

Corbett, D., Wilson, B., & Williams, B. (2002). *Effort and excellence in urban classrooms: Expecting and getting success with all students.* New York: Teachers College Press.

Corcoran, C. A., & Leahy, R. (2003). Growing professionally through reflective practice. *Kappa Delta Pi Record, 40*(1), 30–33.

Corno, L. (2000). Looking at homework differently. *The Elementary School Journal, 100*(5), 529–549.

Cothron, J. H., Giese, R. N., & Rezba, R. J. (1989). *Students and research: Practical strategies for science classrooms and competitions* (2nd ed.). Dubuque, IA: Kendall/Hunt.

Cotton, K. (2000). *The schooling practices that matter most.* Portland, OR: Northwest Regional Educational Laboratory and Alexandria, VA: Association for Supervision and Curriculum Development.

Covino, E. A., & Iwanicki, E. (1996). Experienced teachers: Their constructs on effective teaching. *Journal of Personnel Evaluation in Education, 11,* 325–363.

Cross, C., & Regden, D. W. (2002). Improving teacher quality. *American School Board Journal asbj.com.* Retrieved May 17, 2002, from http://www.absj.com/current/coverstory2.html.

Cruickshank, D. R., & Haefele, D. (2001). Good teachers, plural. *Educational Leadership, 58* (5), 26–30.

Cunningham, P. M., & Allington, R I. (1999). *Classrooms that work: They can all read and write.* New York: Addison-Wesley.

Danielson, C. (2002). *Enhancing student achievement: A framework for school improvement.* Alexandria, VA: Association for Supervision and Curriculum Development.

Danielson, C. (2001). New trends in teacher evaluation. *Educational Leadership, 58*(5), 12–15.

Darling-Hammond, L. (1995). Inequality and access to knowledge. In J. Banks (Ed.), *Handbook of research on multicultural education*. New York: Macmillan.

Darling-Hammond, L. (2000). Teacher quality and student achievement: A review of state policy evidence. *Educational Policy Analysis Archives, 8* (1). Retrieved from http://epaa.asu.edu/epaa/v8n1.

Darling-Hammond, L. (2001). The challenge of staffing our schools. *Educational Leadership, 58*(8), 12–17.

Darling-Hammond, L., Berry, B., & Thoreson, A. (2001). Does teacher certification matter? Evaluating the evidence. *Educational Policy Analysis, 22*(1), 52–57.

Deiro, J. A. (2003). Do your students know you care? *Educational Leadership, 60*(6), 60–62.

Dewitz, P., Carr, E., & Patberg, J. (1989). Using cloze for inference training with expository text. *The Reading Teacher, 42*, 380–385.

Dickson, L. A., & Irving, M. M. (2002). An internet survey: Accessing the extent middle/high school teachers use the internet to enhance science teaching. *Journal of Computers in Mathematics and Science Teaching, 21*(1), 77–96.

Doyle, W. (1986). Classroom organization and management. In M. C. Wittrock (Ed.), *Handbook of research on teaching* (3rd ed., pp. 392–431). New York: Macmillan.

Durall, P. C. (1995). *Years of experience and professional development: A correlation with higher reading scores*. Unpublished doctoral dissertation from Murray State University. (ERIC Document Reproduction Service No. ED386681.)

Edmonton Public Schools. (1993). *Qualities of successful teachers*. Draft Document. Edmonton, Alberta, Canada (May).

Educational Research Service. (2000). Effective classrooms: Teacher behaviors that produce high student achievement. *The Informed Educator Series*. Arlington, VA: Educational Research Service.

Educational Review Office. (1998). *The capable teacher*. Retrieved January 19, 2002, from http://www.ero.govt.nz/Publications/eers1998/98no2hl.html.

Education USA Special Report. (n.d.). *Good teachers: What to look for*. A Publication of The National School Public Relations Association.

Ehrenberg, R. G., & Brewer, D. J. (1995). Did teachers' verbal ability and race matter in the 1960's? Coleman revisited. *Economics of Educational Review, 14*(1), 1–21.

Eisner, E. W. (1999). The uses and limits of performance assessment. *Phi Delta Kappan, 80*(9), 658–660.

Emmer, E. T., Evertson, C. M., & Anderson, L. M. (1980). Effective classroom management at the beginning of the school year. *The Elementary School Journal, 80*(5), 219–231.

Emmer, E. T., Evertson, C. M., & Worsham, M. E. (2003). *Classroom management for secondary teachers*. Boston: Allyn and Bacon.

Entwisle, D. R., & Webster, M., Jr. (1973). Research notes: Status factors in expectation rising. [Electronic version]. *Sociology of Education, 46*, 115–125.

Ferguson, P., & Womack, S. T. (1993). The impact of subject matter and education coursework on teaching performance. *Journal of Teacher Education, 44*(1), 55–63.

Fetler, M. (1999). High school staff characteristics and mathematics test results. *Educational Policy Analysis Archives, 7*(9). Retrieved from http://olam.ed.asu.edu/v7n9.

Fisher, A. L. (2001). Implementing graphic organizer notebooks: The art and science of teaching content. *The Reading Teacher, 55*(2), 116–120.

Fisher, H. L. (2003). Motivational strategies in the elementary school setting. *Kappa Delta Pi Record, 39*(3), 118–121.

Flanders, N. A. (1985). Interaction analysis and clinical supervision. *Journal of Research & Development in Education, 9*(2), 47–57.

Fogarty, R. (2002). *Brain compatible classrooms* (2nd ed.). Arlington Heights, IL: SkyLight Professional Development.

Ford, D. Y., & Trotman, M. F. (2001). Teachers of gifted students: Suggested multicultural characteristics and competencies. *Roper Review, 23*(4), 235–239.

Freel, A. (1998). Achievement in urban schools: What makes the difference? *The Education Digest,* September, 17–22.

Friedl, A. E., & Koontz, T. Y. (2001). *Teaching science to children: An inquiry approach.* Boston: McGraw-Hill.

Fuchs, L. S., Fuchs, D., & Phillips, N. (1994). The relation between teachers' beliefs of the importance of good student work habits, teacher planning, and student achievement. *The Elementary School Journal, 94*(3), 331–345.

Fullan, M. (2000). The three stories of education reform [electronic version]. *Phi Delta Kappan, 81*(8). Retrieved October 30, 2003, from http://www.pdkintl.org/kappan/kful0004.htm.

Gamoran, A., & Nystrand, M. (1992). Taking students seriously. In F. M. Newmann (Ed.), *Student engagement and achievement in American secondary schools.* New York: Teachers College Press.

Gitomer, D. H., Latham, A. S., & Ziomek, R. (1999). *The academic quality of prospective teachers: The impact of admissions and licensure testing.* Retrieved from http://www.ets.org/research/dload/225033.pdf.

Glass, C. S. (2001). Factors influencing teaching strategies used with children who display attention deficit hyperactivity disorder characteristics. *Education, 122*(1), 70–80.

Glass, G. V. (2002). Teacher characteristics. In A. Molnar (Ed.), *School reform proposals: The research evidence.* Retrieved November 4, 2003, from http://www.asu.edu/educ/epsl/EPRU/epru_Research_Writing.htm.

Goe, L. (2002, October 14). Legislating equity: The distribution of emergency permit teachers in California. *Education Policy Analysis Archives, 10*(42). Retrieved from http://epea.asu.edu/epea/v10n42.

Goldhaber, D. D., & Brewer, D. J. (2000). Does teacher certification matter? High school teacher certification status and student achievement. *Educational Evaluation and Policy Analysis, 22*(2), 129–145.

Good, T. L., & Brophy, J. E. (1997). *Looking in classrooms* (7th ed.) New York: Addison-Wesley.

Greenwald, R., Hedges, L., & Laine, R. (1996). The effect of school resources on student achievement. *Review of Educational Research, 66*(3), 361–396.

Gronlund, N. E. (2003). *Assessment of student achievement* (7th ed.). Boston: Allyn and Bacon.

Grossman, P., Valencia, S., Evans, K., Thompson, C., Martin, S., & Place, N. (2000). *Transitions into teaching: Learning to teach writing in teacher education and beyond.* Retrieved November 11, 2003, from http://cela.albany.edu/transitions/main.html.

Guskey, T. R. (1996). Reporting on student learning: Lessons from the past—Prescriptions for the future. *Communicating student learning.* Alexandria, VA: ASCD.

Guskey, T. R. (2002). Does it make a difference? Evaluating professional development. *Educational Leadership, 59*(6), 45–51.

Guskey, T. R. (2003). How classroom assessments improve student learning. *Educational Leadership, 60*(5), 6–11.

Haberman, M. (1995). *STAR teachers of children in poverty.* West Lafayette, IN: Kappa Delta Pi.

Hanushek, E. (1971). Teacher characteristics and gains in student achievement: Estimation using micro data. *American Economic Review, 61*(2), 280–288.

Harris, S. (2003). An andragogical model: Learning through life experiences. *Kappa Delta Pi Record, 40*(1), 38–41.

Hawk, P. P., Coble, C. R., & Swanson, M. (1985). Certification: Does it matter? *Journal of Teacher Education, 36*(3), 13–15.

Haycock, K. (2000). No more settling for less. *Thinking K–16, 4*(1), 3–12.

Higham, W. T., Johnson, M. M., & Gorow, J. (1996). Alternative options study—at the secondary level. Oregon: Office of Curriculum, Instruction, and Field Services-ODE. Retrieved September 9, 2000, from http://www.ode.state.or.us/cifs/alternative/altschre.htm.

Hirsh, E. D. (2000). The tests we need and why we don't quite have them. *Education Week, 19*(21), 40–41, 64.

Hoff, D. J. (2000). U.S. students' scores drop by 8th grade. *Education Week, 20* (15), 1, 20.

Hoff, D. J. (2003, September 3). Large-scale study finds poor math, science instruction. *Education Week, 23* (1), p. 8.

Holahan, P. J., Jurkat, M. P., & Friedman, E. A. (2000). Evaluation of a mentor teacher model for enhancing mathematics instruction through the use of computers [abstract]. *Journal of Research on Technology Education, 32*(3). Retrieved September 22, 2002, from http://www.iste.org/jrte/32/3/abstracts/holahan.html.

Holloway, J. H. (2003). Research link: Sustaining experienced teachers. *Educational Leadership, 60*(8), 87–89.

Hyerle, D. N. (1996). *Visual tools for constructing knowledge.* Alexandria, VA: Association for Supervision and Curriculum Development.

Isaksen, S. G., & Treffinger, D. J. (1985). *Creative problem solving: The basic course.* Buffalo, NY: Bearly Limited.

ISTE. (n.d.). *ISTE research reports: Overview: Research on IT [informational technology] in education.* Retrieved September 22, 2002, from http://www.iste.org/research/reports/tlcu/overview.html.

Jackson, A. W., & Davis, G. A. (with Abeel, M., & Bordonard, A.). (2000). *Turning points 2000: Educating adolescents in the 21st Century.* New York: Teachers College Press.

Jelmberg, J. (1996, January). College based teacher education versus state sponsored alternative programs. *Journal of Teacher Education, 47*(1), 60–66.

Johnson, B. L. (1997). An organizational analysis of multiple perspectives of effective teaching: Implications for teacher evaluation. *Journal of Personnel Evaluation in Education, 11,* 69–87.

Joyce, B., & Showers, B. (1980). Improving inservice training: The messages of research. *Educational Leadership, 37*(5), 379–385.

Jussim, L., & Eccles, J. S. (1992). Teacher expectations II: Construction and reflection of student achievement. *Journal of Personality and Social Psychology, 63*(6), 947–961.

Kalkowski, P. (1995). Peer and cross-age tutoring. *NWREL school improvement research series (SIRS): Research you can use.* Retrieved from http://nwrel.org/scpd/sires/9/c018.html.

Kohn, A. (1996). What to look for in a classroom. *Educational Leadership, (54)*1, 54–55.

Kramer, S. L. (1997). What we know about block scheduling and its effects on math instruction, part I. *NASSP Bulletin, 81*(587), 18–39.

Laczko-Kerr, I., & Berliner, D. C. (2002). The effectiveness of "Teach for America" and other under-certified teachers on student academic achievement: A case of harmful public policy. *Education Policy Analysis Archives, 10*(37). Retrieved November 4, 2003, from http://epaa.asu.edu/epaa/v10n37/.

Langer, J. (2001). Beating the odds: Teaching middle and high school students to read and write well. *American Educational Research Journal, 38*(4), 837–880.

Lewis, C. W., Cobb, R. B., Winokur, M., Leech, N., Viney, M., & White, W. (2003, November 11). The effects of full and alternative day block scheduling on language arts and science achievement in a junior high school. *Education Policy Analysis Archives, 11*(41). Retrieved November 11, 2003, from http://epaa.asu.edu/epaa/v11n41/.

Lin, S. W. (2002). *Improving science teaching through teacher development group: A case study of elementary teachers.* Presented at the annual conference of the National Association for Research in Science Teaching. New Orleans, LA.

Margulies, N. (1991). *Mapping inner space.* Tucson, AZ: Zephyr Press.

Martin, R., Sexton, C., & Gerlovich, J. (2001). *Teaching science for all children* (3rd ed.). Boston: Allyn and Bacon.

Marzano, R. J. (with Marzano, J. S., & Pickering, D. J.). (2003). *Classroom management that works.* Alexandria, VA: Association for Supervision and Curriculum Development.

Marzano, R. J., Norford, J. S., Paynter, D. E., Pickering, D. J., & Gaddy, B. B. (2001). *A handbook for classroom instruction that works.* Alexandria, VA: Association for Supervision and Curriculum Development.

Marzano, R. J., Pickering, D. J., & Pollock, J. E. (2001). *Classroom instruction that works: Research-based strategies for increasing student achievement.* Alexandria, VA: Association for Supervision and Curriculum Development.

Marzano, R. J., Pickering, D., & McTighe, J. (1993). *Assessing student outcomes: Performance assessment using the dimensions of learning model.* Alexandria, VA: Association for Supervision and Curriculum Development.

Mason, D. A., Schroeter, D. D., Combs, R. K., & Washington, K. (1992). Assigning average achieving eighth graders to advanced mathematics classes in an urban junior high. *The Elementary School Journal, 92*(5), 587–599.

Mastropieri, M. A., & Scruggs, T. E. (1991). *Teaching students ways to remember: Strategies for learning mnemonically.* Cambridge, MA: Brookline Books.

McBer, H. (2000). *Research into teacher effectiveness: A model of teacher effectiveness* (Research Report #216). Nottingham, England: Department of Education and Employment.

McEwan, E. K. (2002). *10 traits of highly effective teachers: How to hire, coach, and mentor successful teachers.* Thousand Oaks, CA: Corwin Press.

McKechnie, J. L. (Ed.). (1983). *Webster's new twentieth century dictionary of the English language unabridged* (2nd ed.). New York: Simon and Schuster.

McLeod, J., Fisher, J., & Hoover, G. (2003). *The key elements of classroom management: Managing time and space, student behavior, and instructional strategies.* Alexandria, VA: Association for Supervision and Curriculum Development.

Miller, J. E., McKenna, M. C., & McKenna, B. A. (1998). A comparison of alternatively and traditionally prepared teachers. *Journal of Teacher Education, 49*(3), 165–176.

Monk, D. H. (1994). Subject area preparation of secondary mathematics and science teachers and student achievement. *Economics of Education Review, 13*(2), 125–145.

Nakamura, R. M. (2000). *Healthy classroom management: Motivation, communication, and discipline.* Belmont, CA: Wadsworth.

National Association of Secondary School Principals (NASSP). (1997). Students say: What makes a good teacher? *Schools in the Middle, 6*(5), 15–17.

Noddings, N. (1984). *Caring: A feminine approach to ethics and moral education.* Berkeley, CA: University of California Press.

Noddings, N. (1992). *The challenge to care in schools: An alternative approach to education.* New York: Teachers College Press.

North Carolina Department of Public Instruction. (1999). *Block scheduled high school achievement: Part III comparison of end-of-course test scores for blocked and non-blocked high schools.* Raleigh, NC: Author. Retrieved September 9, 2000, from http://www.dpi.state.nc.us/accountability/evaluation/evalbriefs/vol1n1block-.htm.

NWREL. (2001). *Understanding motivation and supporting teacher renewal.* Retrieved October 20, 2003, from http://www.nwrel.org/nwreport/jan03/motivation.html.

Palinscar, A. S., & Brown, A. L. (1986). Interactive teaching to promote independent reading from text. *Reading Teacher, 39*(8), 771–777.

Panasuk, R., Stone, W., & Todd, J. (2002). Lesson planning strategy for effective mathematics teaching. *Education, 22*(2), 714, 808–827.

Peart, N. A., & Campbell, F. A. (1999). At-risk students' perceptions of teacher effectiveness. *Journal for a Just and Caring Education, 5*(3), 269–284.

Pittelman, S. D., Heimlich, J. E., Berglund, R. L., French, M. P. (1991). *Semantic feature analysis: Classroom applications.* Newark, DE: International Reading Association.

Popham, W. J. (1999). Why standardized tests don't measure educational quality. *Educational Leadership, 56*(6), 8–15.

Popham, W. J. (2002). *Classroom assessment: What teachers need to know* (3rd ed.). Boston: Allyn & Bacon.

Qu, Y., & Becker, B. J. (2003, April). Does traditional teacher certification imply quality? A meta-analysis. Presented at the annual conference of the American Educational Research Association, Chicago, IL.

Readance, J. E., Bean, T. W., & Baldwin, R. S. (1989). *Content area reading* (3rd ed.). Dubuque, IA: Kendall/Hunt.

Reid, B. (1994). *The Copernican timetable and mathematics: Grade 12 exam results at L.V. Rogers Secondary School.* Retrieved September 9, 2000, from http://www.bctf.bc.ca/education/timetables/vector.html.

Reynolds, A. (1992). What is competent beginning teaching? A review of the literature. *Review of Educational Research, 62*(1), 1–35.

Rockwell, R. E., Andre, L. C., & Hawley, M. K. (1996). *Parents and teachers as partners: Issues and challenges.* Fort Worth: Harcourt Brace College.

Roe, B. D., & Ross, E. P. (2002). *Student teaching and field experiences handbook* (5th ed.). Columbus, OH: Merrill Prentice-Hall.

Ross, J. A., Cousins, J. B., Gadalla, T., & Hannay, L. (1999). Administrative assignment of teachers in restructuring secondary schools: The effect of out-of-field course responsibility on teacher efficacy. *Educational Administration Quarterly, 35,* 782–804.

Rowan, B., Chiang, F. S. & Miller, R. J. (1997). Using research on employees' performance to study the effects of teachers on student achievement. *Sociology of Education, 70,* 256–284.

Royce, C. A., & Wiley, D. A. (1996). Children's literature and the teaching of science: Possibilities and cautions. *The Clearinghouse, 70*(1), 18–21.

Sanders, W. L. (2001, January). *The effect of teachers on student achievement.* Keynote address at the Project STARS Institute, Williamsburg, VA.

Sanders, W. L., & Horn, S. P. (1998). Research findings from the Tennessee Value-Added Assessment System (TVAAS) database: Implications for educational evaluation and research. *Journal of Personnel Evaluation in Education, 12,* 247–256.

Santa, C. M., & Havens, L. T. (1991). Learning through writing. In C. M. Santa & D. E. Alverman (Eds.). *Science learning: Processes and applications* (pp. 122–133). Newark, DE: International Reading Association.

Schalock, D., Schalock, M., & Myton, D. (1998). Effectiveness—along with quality—should be the focus. *Phi Delta Kappan, 79*(6), 468–470.

Scherer, M. (2001). Improving the quality of the teaching force: A conversation with David C. Berliner. *Educational Leadership, 58*(8), 6–10.

Schoenstein, R. (1994). Block scheduled: Building the high schools of the future? *Virginia Journal of Education, 88*(3), 7–13.

Schroth, G., & Dixon, J. (1996). The effects of block scheduling on student performance. *International Journal of Educational Reform, 5,* 472–476.

Shellard, E., & Protheroe, N. (2000). Effective teaching: How do we know it when we see it? *The Informed Educator Series.* Arlington, VA: Educational Research Services.

Sizer, T. R. (1999). No two are quite alike. *Educational Leadership, 57* (1), 6–11.

Skrla, L. (2001). The influence of state accountability on teacher expectations and student performance. *UCEA: The Review, 42*(2), 1–4.

Slavin, R. E. (1995). Student teams-achievement divisions in the secondary classroom. In J. E. Petersen and A. D. Digby (Eds.) *Secondary schools and cooperative learning: Theories, models, and strategies* (pp. 425–446). New York: Garland.

Sleeter, C. E. (2001). Preparing teachers for culturally diverse schools. *Journal of Teacher Education, 52*(2), 94–106.

Smith, M. A., & Claxton, D. B. (2003). Using active homework in physical education [electronic version]. *JOPERD, 74*(5), 28–32.

Snyder, D. (1997) *4-block scheduling: A case study of data analysis of one high school after two years.* Angola, IN: Author. Retrieved September 9, 2000, from http://www.msdsteuben.k12.in.us/ahs/stats/mwera.htm.

Sokal, L., Smith, D. G., & Mowat, H. (2003). Alternative certification teachers' attitudes towards classroom management [electronic version]. *High School Journal, 86*(3), 8–16. Retrieved October 30, 2003, from http://80-web5.infotrac.galegroup.com.

Stauffer, R. G. (1969). *Directed reading maturity as a cognitive process.* New York: Harper & Row.

Staunton, J. (1997). A study of teacher beliefs on the efficacy of block scheduling. *NASSP Bulletin, 81*(593), 73–80.

Stiggins, R. J. (2002). Assessment crisis: The absence of assessment for learning [electronic version]. *Phi Delta Kappan, 83*(10). Retrieved October 30, 2003, from http://80-web2.infotrac.galegroup.com.

Strauss, R. P., & Sawyer, E. A. (1986). Some new evidence on teacher and student competencies. *Economics of Education Review, 5*(1), 41–48.

Stronge, J. H. (2002). *Qualities of effective teachers.* Alexandria, VA: Association for Supervision and Curriculum Development.

Stronge, J. H., Tucker, P. D., & Ward, T. J. (2003, April). *Teacher effectiveness and student learning: What do good teachers do?* Presented at the American Educational Research Association. Chicago, IL.

Swap, S. A. (1993). *Developing home-school partnerships from concepts to practice.* New York: Teachers College Press.

Taylor, B. M., Pearson, P. D., Clark, K. F., & Walpole, S. (1999). Center for the improvement of early reading achievement: Effective schools/accomplished teachers. *The Reading Teacher, 53*(2), 156–159.

Texas Education Agency Office of Policy Planning and Research Division of Research and Evaluation. (1999, September). *Block scheduling in Texas public high schools* (Report No. 13). Austin, TX: Author.

Thier, M., & Daviss, B. (2002). *The new science literacy: Using language skills to help students learn science.* Portsmouth, NH: Heinemann.

Thomas B. Fordham Foundation. (1999). *The teachers we need and how to get more of them.* Retrieved August 26, 2001, from http://www.edexcellence.net/library/teacher.html.

Thomas, J. A., & Montgomery, P. (1998). On becoming a good teacher: Reflective practice with regard to children's voices. *Journal of Teacher Education, 49*(5), 372–380.

Thompson, J. G. (2002). *First-year teacher's survival kit.* San Francisco, CA: Jossey-Bass.

Tobin, K. (1980). The effect of extended teacher wait-time on science achievement. *Journal of Research in Science Teaching, 17,* 469–475.

Tomlinson, C. A. (1999). *The differentiated classroom: Responding to the needs of all learners.* Alexandria, VA: Association for Supervision and Curriculum Development.

Totten, S. (1995). Jigsaw synthesis: A method for incorporating a study of social issues into the extant curriculum. In J. E. Petersen and A. D. Digby (Eds.) *Secondary schools and cooperative learning: Theories, models, and strategies* (pp. 389–424). New York: Garland.

Tschannen-Moran, M., & Hoy, W. K. (2000). A multidisciplinary analysis of the nature, meaning, and measurement of trust. *Review of Educational Research, 70*(4), 547–593.

Veal, W. R., & Schreiber, J. (1999). Block scheduling effects on a state mandated test of basic skills. *Education Policy Analysis Archives, 7*(29). Retrieved October 12, 2000, from http://epaa.asu.edu/epaa/v7n29.html.

Virginia Department of Education (VDOE). (2001, April). *WordsAlive.* Presentation at Christopher Newport University, Newport News, VA.

Walberg, H. J. (1984). Improving the productivity of America's schools. *Educational Leadership, 41*(8), 19–27.

Walker, M. H. (1998). 3 basics for better student output. *Education Digest, 63*(9), 15–18.

Wang, M., Haertel, G. D., & Walberg, H. (1993/1994). What helps students learn? *Educational Leadership, 51*(4), 74.

Wasserman, S. (1999). Shazam! You're a teacher: Facing the illusory quest for certainty in classroom practice. *Phi Delta Kappan, 80*(6), 464-468.

Wasserstein, P. (1995). What middle schoolers say about their school work. *Educational Leadership, 53*(1), 41–43.

Watson, S. M. R., & Houtz, L. E. (2002). Teaching science: Meeting the academic needs of culturally and linguistically diverse learners [electronic version]. *Intervention in School and Clinic, 37*(5), 267–278.

Wayne, A. J., & Youngs, P. (2003). Teacher characteristics and student achievement gains: A review. *Review of Educational Research, 73*(1), 89–122.

Weiss, I. R., Pasley, J. D., Smith, P. S., Banilower, E. R., & Heck, D. J. (2003). *Looking inside the classroom: A study of K–12 mathematics and science education in the United States.* Retrieved December 10, 2003, from www.horizon-research.com/insidetheclassroom/reports/looking/complete.pdf.

Wellington, J. J., & Osborne, J. (2001). *Language and literacy in science education.* Philadelphia: Open University Press.

Wenglinsky, H. (2000). *How teaching matters: Bringing the classroom back into discussions of teacher quality* Princeton, NJ: Millikan Family Foundation and Educational Testing Service.

Wenglinsky, H. (2002). How schools matter: The link between teacher classroom practices and student academic performance. *Educational Policy Analysis Archives, 10*(12). Retrieved February 28, 2002, from http://epaa.asu.edu/epaa/v10n12/.

Wharton-McDonald, R., Pressley, M., & Hampston, J. M. (1998). Literacy instruction in nine first-grade classrooms: Teacher characteristics and student achievement [electronic version]. *The Elementary School Journal, 99*(2). Retrieved October 30, 2003, from http://80-web3.infotrac.galegroup.com.proxy.wm.edu/itw/infomark/993/701/64058160w3/purl=rc1_EAIM_0_A54851458&dyn=4!ar_fmt?sw_aep=viva_wm.

Wolk, S. (2002). *Being good: Rethinking classroom management and student discipline.* Portsmouth, NH: Heinemann.

Wolk, S. (2003). Hearts and minds. *Educational Leadership, 61*(1), 14–18.

Woolfolk-Hoy, A. W., & Hoy, W. K. (2003). *Instructional leadership: A learning-centered guide.* Boston: Allyn and Bacon.

Wright, S. P., Horn, S. P., & Sanders, W. L. (1997). Teacher and classroom context effects on student achievement: Implications for teacher evaluation. *Journal of Personnel Evaluation in Education, 11*, 57–67.

Wronkovich, M., Hess, C. A., & Robinson, J. E. (1997). An objective look at math outcomes based on new research into block scheduling. *NASSP Bulletin, 81*(593), 32–41.

Wubbels, T., Levy, J., & Brekelmans, M. (1997). Paying attention to relationships (electronic version). *Educational Leadership, 54*(7), 82–86. Retrieved November 12, 2003, from http://pdonline.ascd.org/pd_online/classmanage/e1199704_wubbels.html.

Ysseldyke, J., & Wiltse, P. (n. d.). *Strategies and tactics for effective instruction.* Retrieved May 18, 2003, from http://education.umn.edu/CI/MREA/EffectInst/effectiveMODtoc.html.

Zahorik, J., Halbach, A., Ehrle, K., & Molnar, A. (2003). Teaching practices for smaller classes. *Educational Leadership, 61*(1), 75–77.

INDEX

Note: Page numbers followed by *f* refer to figures.

ABOUT THE AUTHORS

James H. Stronge is Heritage Professor in the Educational Policy, Planning, and Leadership Area at the College of William and Mary in Williamsburg, Virginia. Among his primary research interests are teacher effectiveness and student success, and teacher and administrator performance evaluation. He has worked with many school districts and state and national educational organizations to design and develop evaluation systems for teachers, administrators, superintendents, and support personnel. He is the author or co-author of numerous articles, books, and technical reports on teacher quality and performance evaluation. Selected authored, co-authored, and edited books include:

- ▲ *Handbook on Educational Specialist Evaluation* (Eye on Education, 2003),
- ▲ *Superintendent Evaluation Handbook* (Scarecrow Press, 2003),
- ▲ *Handbook on Teacher Evaluation* (Eye on Education, 2003),
- ▲ *Qualities of Effective Teaching* (Association for Supervision and Curriculum Development, 2002),
- ▲ *Handbook on Teacher Portfolios for Evaluation and Professional Development* (Eye on Education, 2000),
- ▲ *Teacher Evaluation and Student Achievement* (National Education Association, 2000),
- ▲ *Evaluating Teaching: A Guide to Current Thinking and Best Practice* (Corwin Press, 1997), and

▲ *Evaluating Professional Support Personnel in Education* (Sage Publications, 1991).

He received his doctorate in the area of educational administration and planning from the University of Alabama. Stronge has been a teacher, counselor, and district-level administrator. He can be contacted at: The College of William and Mary, School of Education, P.O. Box 8795, Williamsburg, VA 23187-8795, 757-221-2339, or jhstro@wm.edu.

Pamela D. Tucker is an associate professor of education in the Curry School of Education at the University of Virginia, Charlottesville, where she serves as the director of the Principal Internship Program. Her research focuses on teacher effectiveness, the nature of the school principalship, and personnel evaluation. Books coauthored with others include: *Handbook on Teacher Portfolios for Evaluation and Professional Development* (Eye on Education), *Educational Leadership in an Age of Accountability* (SUNY Press), *Handbook on Teacher Evaluation: Assessing and Improving Performance*, *Handbook on Educational Specialist Evaluation: Assessing and Improving Performance* (Eye on Education), and *Teacher Evaluation and Student Achievement* (National Education Association). Her articles address topics including teacher portfolios, helping struggling teachers, guidelines for linking student achievement and teacher evaluation, and the legal context for teacher evaluation. She has worked with numerous school districts and the Commonwealth of Virginia to design evaluation systems for teachers, administrators, and support personnel. She earned her Ed.D. in Educational Administration from the College of William and Mary. She has been a middle school teacher, special education teacher, and school administrator.

Jennifer L. Hindman is an educational consultant in the areas of teacher effectiveness; teacher, educational specialist, and administrator performance evaluation; and teacher selection. Her work has been published by *Educational Leadership* and the National Center for Homeless Education. Her research interests include teacher effectiveness and teacher selection. She has conducted numerous workshops on enhancing teacher effectiveness in science. She also works as an Outreach Specialist for Project HOPE, Virginia's McKinney-Vento state program for ensuring the educational rights of students experiencing homelessness. She earned her Ph.D. in Educational Policy, Planning, and Leadership at the College of William and Mary. She has been a middle school teacher and a science specialist.

Related ASCD Resources

At the time of publication, the following ASCD resources were available; for the most up-to-date information about ASCD resources, go to http://www.ascd.org. ASCD stock numbers are noted in parentheses.

Networks

Visit the ASCD Web site (http://www.ascd.org) and search for "networks" for information about professional educators who have formed groups around topics such as "Affective Factors in Learning," "Mentoring Leadership and Resources," and "Performance Assessment for Leadership." Look in the "Network Directory" for current facilitators' addresses and phone numbers.

Print Products

A Better Beginning: Supporting and Mentoring New Teachers by Marge Scherer (#199236)

Classroom Instruction That Works: Research-Based Strategies for Increasing Student Achievement by Robert J. Marzano, Debra J. Pickering, and Jane E. Pollock (#101010)

Enhancing Professional Practice: A Framework for Teaching by Charlotte Danielson (#196074)

Grading and Reporting Student Learning by Robert J. Marzano and Tom Guskey (Professional Inquiry Kit; # 901061)

A Handbook for Classroom Instruction That Works by Robert J. Marzano, Jennifer S. Norford, Diane E. Paynter, Debra J. Pickering, and Barbara B. Gaddy (#101041)

How to Help Beginning Teachers Succeed, 2nd ed., by Stephen P. Gordon and Susan Maxey (#100217)

Teacher Evaluation/Teacher Portfolios ASCD Electronic Topic Pack (#197202)

A Teacher's Guide to Working with Paraeducators and Other Classroom Aides by Jill Morgan and Betty Y. Ashbaker (#100236)

Videotapes

The Teacher Series (two sets of 3 tapes each) (#401088, #401089)

For more information, visit us on the World Wide Web (http://www.ascd.org), send an e-mail message to member@ascd.org, call the ASCD Service Center (1-800-933-ASCD or 703-578-9600, then press 2), send a fax to 703-575-5400, or write to Information Services, ASCD, 1703 N. Beauregard St., Alexandria, VA 22311-1714 USA.